Models of Premillennialism

Models of Premillennialism

Sung Wook Chung
David Mathewson

FOREWORD BY
Craig Blomberg

CASCADE *Books* · Eugene, Oregon

MODELS OF PREMILLENNIALISM

Copyright © 2018 Sung Wook Chung and David Mathewson. All rights reserved. Except for brief quotations in critical publications or reviews, no part of this book may be reproduced in any manner without prior written permission from the publisher. Write: Permissions, Wipf and Stock Publishers, 199 W. 8th Ave., Suite 3, Eugene, OR 97401.

Cascade Books
An Imprint of Wipf and Stock Publishers
199 W. 8th Ave., Suite 3
Eugene, OR 97401

www.wipfandstock.com

PAPERBACK ISBN: 978-1-5326-3769-8
HARDCOVER ISBN: 978-1-5326-3770-4
EBOOK ISBN: 978-1-5326-3771-1

Cataloguing-in-Publication data:

Names: Chung, Sung Wook, 1966–, author. | Mathewson, David, author. | Blomberg, Craig L., 1955–, foreword writer.

Title: Models of premillennialism / Sung Wook Chung and David Mathewson, with a foreword by Craig Blomberg.

Description: Eugene, OR: Cascade Books, 2018 | Includes bibliographical references and index.

Identifiers: ISBN 978-1-5326-3769-8 (paperback) | ISBN 978-1-5326-3770-4 (hardcover) | ISBN 978-1-5326-3771-1 (ebook)

Subjects: LCSH: Eschatology | Millennialism | Millennium (Eschatology)—History of Doctrines | Dispensationalism | Theology—Asia

Classification: BT892 C37 2018 (print) | BT892 (ebook)

Manufactured in the U.S.A.   08/24/18

Content

Foreword by Craig Blomberg | vii
Introduction | xi

1. Historic Premillennialism | 1
2. Classical Dispensational Premillennialism | 30
3. Progressive Dispensationalism | 53
4. Thematic Millennialism | 70
5. Historic Premillennialism in South Korea | 88

   Concluding Reflections on Premillennialism | 119

   Bibliography | 127
   Author Index | 133
   Scripture Index | 135

Foreword

VIEWS OF THE END times or last days of human history as we know it prove perennially fascinating. One of the reasons for this seems to be the recurring pattern of those who confidently announce the date and timing of Christ's return. After two thousand years of this practice, it is not likely to stop any time soon. When my generation of baby boomers were young adults, many of us became frustrated with the hegemony of old-line dispensationalism, with its emphasis on saving souls without caring for their bodies in this life. Millennials today at times have to be persuaded that discussions about differing views of eschatology are worth any time at all. They have imbibed the emphasis on social justice that we renewed a generation ago, sometimes at the expense of evangelism altogether. But all it takes is a compelling writer like Joel Rosenberg (or a pair of writers like Tim LaHaye and Jerry Jenkins) and the fascination returns. A cluster of "natural" disasters combined with an unusual flurry of particularly traumatic public events, preferably in the Middle East, and people of all ages begin asking the question afresh: "is this the threshold of the end?"

When Sung Wook Chung and I eight years ago edited our book, *A Case for Historic Premillennialism* (Grand Rapids: Baker, 2009), we surprised even the publisher with the amount of interest it garnered. Many people had heard of historic (or classic) premillennialism but knew very little about how it differed from dispensational premillennialism and why, much less how to evaluate its strengths and weaknesses. But dispensational eschatology has gone through multiple phases during its short history since 1830 and historic premillennialism has spawned offshoot perspectives as well, which makes a volume like this one most welcome.

The whole Calvinist-Reformed-Presbyterian wing of Reformation or Protestant Christianity has typically been amillennial. But it was only a little over a decade ago that I learned that a large percentage of Asian, and especially Korean, Presbyterian thought preferred historic premillennialism to dispensational premillennialism. I was privileged to participate in an international conference in Seoul in 2012 attended by hundreds of conferees, most of them pastors, on historic premillennialism. I would not have guessed there would be not merely the interest but the electricity in the air surrounding the group of speakers on this topic, including Dr. Chung and me. It was a good reminder that historical and cultural factors in a given part of the world can make a given doctrine of the Christian faith become a topic of great interest when believers elsewhere struggle to see why it should be so important.

Dispensationalism has arguably remained as strong as it has in North America, and in parts of the world influenced by the active missionary movements spawned by dispensationalist colleges and seminaries (esp. Dallas Theological Seminary and Moody Bible Institute), because of Americans' obsession with the avoidance of suffering. My counseling colleagues and my friends who are practicing professional counselors routinely tell me that North American theologies of suffering are downright anemic, and my own teaching experience in college, seminary, and church settings confirms that many who opt for dispensationalism's pretribulational rapture do so not because they can defend it exegetically but because they simply want it to be true. Then, if they are alive at the time of the rapture, they can count on getting out of at least the worst of human suffering. On the other hand, those who adopt a posttribulational rapture occasionally have almost a survivalist mentality and envision stockpiling supplies for the days of persecution to come and weapons to ward off all those who would come to try to take those supplies from them!

FOREWORD

What does the Bible really teach? What do each of the various forms of historic and dispensational premillennialism actually maintain? What are the most significant texts for each school of thought? What are the strengths and weaknesses of each? How does a person decide which to adopt? Although there have been helpful books published to aid readers in choosing among premillennialism, postmillennialism, and amillennialism, and though short sections of larger books on eschatology or systematic theology more generally have at times subdivided the positions further with brief comments on each, a book with substantial chapters of five main forms of premillennial thought, or the millennialism it has spawned, has heretofore never appeared (unless privately published somewhere with very limited exposure). That fact alone makes Chung and Mathewson's volume crucially needed.

Both authors are uniquely equipped to contribute to this volume. Dr. Chung was raised in Korea, but trained in Europe and America for his highest degrees. Eschatology has always been a particular interest of his within his discipline of systematic theology and he has remained closely in touch with the developments in numerous Asian countries, including a number where he has taught, and especially in Korea where he returns for research and ministry every summer. Dr. Mathewson was raised in an old-line dispensationalist context in the U.S., but studied in the U.K. for his New Testament doctorate, specializing in the book of Revelation, and has numerous book- and article-length publications on eschatology and apocalyptic. Together they offer a very accessible introduction, demonstrating that there is far more than one form of premillennialism and that not all premillennialisms are created equal. I count it a privilege that both men are colleagues of mine as members of the full-time faculty of Denver Seminary as well as good friends. I am happy to commend this volume most warmly to the wide readership it deserves.

Craig L. Blomberg, November 2017

Introduction

IN ESCHATOLOGICAL DISCUSSION, PREMILLENNIALISM has been one of the key views on the table throughout church history, and indeed is the earliest Christian position on the matter of the millennium, though even early on other views vied for attention. However, premillennialist interpretations of the last things of human history have not taken a monolithic trajectory, but rather demonstrated a variety of options that compete with one another to attract their adherents. The relevant text, the only place where a millennium is explicitly mentioned in Scripture, is Revelation 20:4–6:

> [4]I saw thrones on which were seated those who had been given authority to judge. And I saw the souls of those who had been beheaded because of their testimony about Jesus and because of the word of God. They had not worshiped the beast or its image and had not received the mark on their foreheads or their hands. They came to life and reigned with Christ a thousand years. [5](The rest of the dead did not come to life until the thousand years were ended.) This is the first resurrection. [6]Blessed and holy are those who share in the first resurrection. The second death has no power over them, but they will be priests of God and of Christ and will reign with him for a thousand years.

All approaches to the millennium are ultimately based on how one factors in this difficult text. However, what all premillennial views have in common, and what distinguishes them from other millennial views (amillennial, postmillennial), is that the millennium of Revelation 20:4–6 is a period of time that 1) is still future and 2) is initiated only by the second coming of Jesus Christ. The first element (and the second, which follows naturally) in particular distinguishes premillennial views from amillennialism. With amillennialism in its different forms, the millennium is not a future period of time, but symbolizes the entire period of time between the first and second comings of Christ. That is, it has already been inaugurated with the death and resurrection of Christ. In contrast to this, premillennial views have in common that the millennium in Revelation 20:1–6 will only be inaugurated in the future, with the second coming of Christ. Premillennial views will read all of Revelation 19–20 as a series of events that transpire only at the second coming of Christ.

The second element, that the millennium is only initiated at the second coming of Christ distinguishes premillennialism clearly from postmillennialism. This latter view shares with premillennialism that the millennium of Revelation 20:1–6 is still future, but it differs in that postmillennialism sees the millennium as a "golden age" initiated by the witnessing activity of the church and the Holy Spirit through the spread of the gospel prior to the second coming of Christ (hence *post*millennialism—Christ returns *following* the millennium). By contrast, premillennial approaches insist that the millennium follows, or is inaugurated by, the second coming of Christ. Once more, premillennialism would interpret Revelation 19–20 as a series of events that transpire only as a result of the second coming of Christ to earth.

But as already noted, not all premillennial views are the same! We tend to think of premillennialism as a rather monolithic viewpoint, or perhaps as only offering a couple of options (dispensational, historical premillennialism). On the basis of these initial insights, this book is an attempt to explore and expound five major proposals aligned with premillennialist construals of scriptural revelation of the last things, particularly Revelation 20:4–6. The first chapter expounds historic premillennialism, which is

INTRODUCTION

the most ancient version of premillennialism and has numerous proponents among theologians, pastors, and ordinary Christians throughout the history of the church. Chapter 2 deals with classical dispensational premillennialism, which has been considerably and consistently popular among fundamentalists and conservative evangelicals ever since its inception in Great Britain in the nineteenth century. Chapter 3 discusses progressive dispensationalism, which some major dispensationalists have recently proposed in response to legitimate critiques of classical dispensational premillennialism in relation to its hermeneutical lopsidedness and privileging the Jews over the gentiles without paying a proper attention to the continuity of God's dealings with both groups of people.

The fourth chapter explores thematic premillennialism, which presents creative interpretations of the millennium without compromising its premillennialist commitment. The fifth chapter presents a discussion of historic premillennialism interpreted and construed in an Asian context, focusing on eschatological discussion among Korean exegetical scholars. Finally, the current authors provide concluding reflections on premillennialism so that the readers can continue to study the theme on their own with the appropriate discernment. We have authored this book not merely for other professional scholars but also for seminary students, local church pastors, and theologically serious lay people.

Special thanks go to Craig Blomberg who wrote the foreword and gave us invaluable feedback on the first draft of the essays.

Thanksgiving 2017

Sung Wook Chung
David L. Mathewson

1

Historic Premillennialism

—Sung Wook Chung

Introduction

IN THIS CHAPTER WE will examine historic premillennialism, focusing on its hermeneutical principles, major tenets, and origins, as well as its development throughout the history of Western Christianity. Historic premillennialism is a rich view with a profound legacy and tradition within the church. It is certainly not an overstatement to conclude that most evangelical theologians today hold to the historic premillennial view. It is widely accepted that the majority of professionally trained evangelical theologians espouse the historic premillennial view and judge it to be the most faithful among the millennial views to the teaching of the Bible. It is hard to determine whether that scholarly majority consists of 50 percent, 60 percent, or 70 percent of the trained professionals, but it is no small thing that a perceivable majority of trained biblical and systematic theologians align themselves with the historic premillennial view. For instance, Roger Olson, a professor of historical theology at Baylor University, commented on this matter in his endorsement of *A Case for Historic Premillennialism: An Alternative to "Left Behind" Eschatology*, which the current author co-edited with Craig L. Blomberg: "It's about time we had a scholarly presentation and defense of historic premillennialism, which is probably the majority view of the 'end times' among theologically trained evangelicals.... If read carefully by many, it will turn the growing tide of 'pretrib rapturism' and restore the eschatology of the Bible and the church fathers."[1]

While dispensationalism finds overwhelming support from the public, historic premillennialism continues to be the dominant view among evangelical scholars. These scholars agree that this view remains closest to the text of Scripture and, moreover, serves as the most biblically sound view of eschatology. Here, I intend to corroborate this argument with various sources of evidence. In the first section of this chapter, I will examine the hermeneutical principles and fundamental tenets of historic premillennialism. In the second section, I will engage critically with historic premillennialism, delving into some of its difficulties and demerits. In the third section, I will explore the two-thousand-year history of the Christian church and trace the origins and the developments of the historic premillennial view. In the fourth section, I will investigate the standing of historic premillennialism in the twentieth- and twenty-first-century Western evangelical camp. In the final section, I will summarize the key points of my argument and suggest a number of ways in which current studies of the book of Revelation and biblical eschatology can advance in the future.

Hermeneutical Principles and Fundamental Tenets

Literal and Futurist Interpretation of Revelation 20:1–6

One of the most important hermeneutical principles of historic premillennialism is its literal, futurist interpretation of Revelation 20, which describes the millennial kingdom. This is closely connected with a rejection of symbolic and spiritual readings of the chapter, which have been dominant in both amillennial and postmillennial circles. Verses 1–3 tell us that an angel from heaven will seize the dragon, that ancient serpent who is the devil, or Satan, and bind him for a thousand years. The angel will

1. Blomberg and Chung, eds., *Case for Historic Premillennialism.*

throw him into the abyss, and lock and seal it over him. Satan will be kept from deceiving the nations anymore until the thousand years will be ended. After the thousand years, Satan must be set free for a short time.

In addition, vv. 4–6 tell us that those have been given authority to judge will be seated on thrones. Those who have been beheaded and have not worshiped the beast or its image will come back to life and reign with Christ for a thousand years. There are still scholarly debates and disputes over who these people are. Many scholars argue that these will be all true Christians, including martyrs. Other scholars contend that these will be martyrs alone who have been killed not only throughout church history but also during the great tribulation right before the parousia.[2]

Nevertheless, from the perspective of a literal, futurist interpretation of this passage, it is crystal clear that those who will experience the first resurrection will reign with Christ for a thousand years. The second death will have no power over them and they will be priests of God and of Christ. For historic premillennialists, this passage must be interpreted in a plain sense, not symbolically or spiritually, as most amillennialists and postmillennialists have interpreted it. Moreover, this passage must be interpreted from the futurist, not preterist, perspective. For example, most amillennialists argue that the binding of Satan in v. 2 is symbolic of the defeat of Satan that occurred when Jesus Christ was crucified for our sin and resurrected from the dead for our righteousness. Historic premillennialists view the symbolic and preterist interpretation of the passage to be groundless because the devil is *still* prowling "around like a roaring lion looking for someone to devour" (1 Pet 5:8). According to 1 Peter 5:8, Satan seems not completely bound but rather still very active in devouring and deceiving people.

---

2. Mounce, *Book of Revelation*, 345–78; Fee, *Revelation*, 279–83.

Chronological Interpretation of Revelation 19–20

For historic premillennialists, the literal and futurist interpretation of Revelation 20:1–6 is closely connected with the chronological interpretation of Revelation 19–20. Most interpreters of the book of Revelation, including those committed to historic premillennialism, concur that Revelation 19 talks about the second coming of the Lord Jesus Christ. In particular, vv. 19–21 of this chapter tell us that both the beast and the false prophet will be captured and thrown alive into the fiery lake of burning sulfur. So two members of the evil trinity, not including Satan, have already been thrown into the lake of fire by chapter 20.

After the depiction of the Lord's second coming in Revelation 19, 20:1–6 describes the millennial reign of Christ and his saints. According to vv. 7–10, after the millennial kingdom, Satan will be released to deceive the nations in the four corners of the earth. Many will be deceived and will participate in Satan's attempt to attack the city of God's people. But they will be devoured by the fire from heaven. And then the devil will be "thrown into the lake of burning sulfur, where the beast and the false prophet had been thrown" (v. 10). This is the description of the final destiny of Satan. It is very important to note here that when the devil was thrown into the lake of fire, he found the beast and the false prophet there, who had already been thrown before him.[3]

This strongly implies that there is a *chronological order* among these three crucial eschatological events, namely, the parousia of chapter 19, the millennium of 20:1–6, and Satan's final judgment of 20:7–10.

Posttribulational Rapture: The Church Suffers through the Tribulation

Most historic premillennialists advocate a *post*tribulational rapture rather than a *pre*tribulational rapture. This means that there will be

---

[3]. For an excellent exposition in line with the present authors' arguments, see Blomberg, "Posttribulationism of the New Testament," 61–88.

a period of great tribulation before the parousia and that the church will suffer through the tribulation rather than be suddenly raptured beforehand, as dispensational premillennialism contends.[4]

Historic premillennialists present multiple biblical passages as evidence for a posttribulational rapture. The most powerful example is Revelation 13:10, which states, "'If anyone is to go into captivity, into captivity they will go. If anyone is to be killed with the sword, with the sword they will be killed. This calls for patient endurance and faithfulness on the part of God's people." This passage teaches clearly that God's people—that is, the church—should endure the tribulation with patience and faithfulness. Of course, dispensationalists would interpret "God's people" here to be the left-behind Jews. It is important, however, to note that the book of Revelation is intended not for the Jews but for the churches (Rev 22:16). So "God's people" in chapter 13 should be construed as churches rather than ethnic Jews.

Two Resurrections

Historic premillennialists believe that there will be two resurrections of humanity. The first resurrection will occur when the Lord comes again publicly after the great tribulation in order to establish his earthly millennial kingdom. The deceased saints, including all martyrs, will be resurrected and raptured to welcome the Lord in the sky. Then they will come down to earth and enter the millennial kingdom. The second resurrection will occur at the end of the millennium before the great white throne judgment. All nonbelievers will be raised again for final judgment. Therefore, there are two separate resurrections, one for the righteous dead and the other for the unrighteous dead, with the gap of the millennium between them. Of course, there are still some disputes among historic premillennialists about these resurrections, as we will discuss later. Nevertheless, it is safe to say that the majority

---

4. The most powerful defense of the posttribulational rapture view is Ladd, *Blessed Hope*.

view among historic premillennialists is that the two resurrections will occur before and after the millennial kingdom.

Millennial Kingdom on Earth: Penultimate State

Most historic premillennialists argue that the millennial kingdom will be established on earth right after the parousia as the *pen*ultimate state of the world before the consummation of the kingdom, the coming of the new heaven and the new earth. The rationale for such an interpretation is that the physical, spatio-temporal paradise must be restored to the present, existing earth before the dawn of the eternalized and glorified cosmos, which Scripture calls "the new heaven and the new earth."

Another rationale for this interpretation is grounded upon Adam christology. Before the fall, Adam was blessed and commissioned to rule over the earth (Gen 1:26–28), expanding his dominion beyond the Garden of Eden to the whole earth. Tragically, however, Adam fell from his original state through disobedience and lost the original blessings God had given him. Despite the fall of Adam, God promised that "the seed of the woman" would come and crush the head of the serpent (Gen 3:15), which implies that the last Adam, Jesus Christ, would restore the kingdom and dominion originally given to Adam. God will fulfill his original promise to establish Adam's kingdom on earth through the second man, Jesus Christ. Through this process, God's original plan and purpose for this earth will be fulfilled. After the millennial kingdom ends, the new heaven and the new earth, the eternalized and glorified cosmos, will come as the ultimate consummation of God's eternal plan and economy.[5]

Who, then, will enter the millennial kingdom? According to the traditional historic premillennial perspective, it is the resurrected and transformed believers who will enter and reign with the Lord Jesus in the millennial kingdom. In addition, the nonbelievers who are alive at the parousia will enter the millennium with

---

5. I discuss this theme in detail in my article, "Toward the Reformed and Covenantal Theology of Premillennialism," 133–46.

their natural bodies and will be subjected to the rule of Christ and the resurrected and transformed saints. These nonbelievers will continue to reproduce, giving birth to their descendants, some of whom will rebel against God, having been deceived by Satan when he is released at the end of the millennium.

Critical Engagement

The present authors believe that historic premillennialism is the millennial view most faithful to Scripture. In particular, the posttribulational view of the rapture seems to be correct on the basis of a faithful exegesis of relevant texts. However, there are still some debatable issues in relation to historic premillennialism. One of the most pressing questions is whether the millennial kingdom will be literally a thousand-years long or a relatively short period. Another dispute is connected with the question of whether nonbelievers will enter the millennium. Will they not be judged and destroyed completely through the arbitration of the Lord Jesus? Or will only the soldiers be killed? There are different and mutually exclusive proposals to these questions, even among historic premillennialists. Historic premillennialists have never been successful in constructing a consensus in relation to these seemingly complex and complicated issues. For that reason, some have rejected premillennialism in favor of the amillennialist perspective, which appears to be simpler and more straightforward.

Historic Premillennialism throughout Church History

The Age of the Early Church and Church Fathers (First to Fourth Centuries AD)

Anyone who has studied church history knows that most of the early church fathers held the historic premillennial view of the end times. Such was the tendency of the church since the first century AD, during and after the death of the apostle John, who wrote the book of Revelation. This fact is uncontested by most church historians.[6]

Polycarp (69–155)

A person of special interest for our purposes is Polycarp, a disciple of the apostle John and the Christian bishop of Smyrna in the late first century AD. Evidence leads us to believe that Polycarp actively taught and preached on a literal great tribulation and a literal millennial kingdom on earth at the second coming of Christ. We are not able to evince this from the preserved works of Polycarp himself, but the fact that his contemporaries and other disciples of John markedly taught the historic premillennial view strongly suggests that Polycarp held the historic premillennial view as well. For example, as we will demonstrate later, Papias was another disciple of John who taught the historic premillennial standpoint. Polycarp's disciple Irenaeus also advocated the historic premillennial view. The fact that the apostle John, Polycarp's own teacher, and Irenaeus, his disciple, both taught the characteristically historic premillennial view leads us to safely speculate that Polycarp also subscribed to and taught the foundational tenets of historic premillennialism.

Papias (ca. 70–155)

Papias was another disciple of the apostle John and was the second-century bishop of Hierapolis in Phrygia. As a leader of the early church, Papias markedly emphasized in his teaching the great tribulation, the appearance of the Antichrist, the second coming of Jesus, and the thousand-year earthly reign of the saints after the second coming. Papias asserted that "there will be a period of a thousand years after the resurrection from the dead when the kingdom of Christ will be set up in material form on

---

6. Lewis and Demarest, *Integrative Theology*, 3:377. See Fairbairn, "Contemporary Millennial/Tribulational Debates," 105–32.

this earth."⁷ This and other similar teachings establish Papias as the first bishop to explicitly articulate the historic premillennial view since the apostle John.

Papias gave the following very detailed and interesting depiction of the millennial kingdom: "The days will come when vines will grow, each having ten thousand shoots, and on each shoot ten thousand branches, and on each branch ten thousand twigs, and on each twig ten thousand clusters, and in each cluster ten thousand grapes, and each grape when crusted will yield twenty-five measures of wine."⁸ Of course, there is no scriptural evidence that substantiates this precise depiction, but we can gather from this that Papias understood the millennial kingdom to be an actual earthly kingdom that communicates God's divine restoration of the created world in the last days.

Justin Martyr (103–65)

Justin Martyr was a contemporary of Polycarp and Papias in the mid-second century who had massive influence as a Christian apologist. He also emphasized the second coming of Jesus and taught that "[t]he Prophets have proclaimed two advents of [Christ]: the [first] one, that which is already past, when he came as a dishonored and suffering man; but the second, when according to prophecy, he shall come from heaven with glory, accompanied by his angelic host."⁹ Regarding the Antichrist's persecution of the believers during the great tribulation, Justin wrote, "[Christ] will come from heaven with glory, when the man of apostasy, who speaks strange things against the most High, shall venture to do unlawful deeds on the earth against us Christians."¹⁰ He further asserted the following regarding the post-return establishment of the earthly millennial kingdom: "I and others who are right-minded

---

7. *Fragments of Papias* 3.12, in Holmes, *Apostolic Fathers*, 567.
8. *Fragments of Papias* 14.2, in Holmes, *Apostolic Fathers*, 581.
9. Justin Martyr, *First Apology* 52, in *ANF* 1:180.
10. Justin Martyr, *Dialogue with Trypho* 110, in *ANF* 1:253–54.

Christians on all points, are assured that there will be a resurrection of the dead and a thousand years in Jerusalem, which will then be built, adorned, and enlarged."[11] It is clear that the eschatological convictions of Justin Martyr best align with the historic premillennial view. According to Gordon Lewis and Bruce Demarest, Justin Martyr is known to have claimed that all Christian leaders of the second century, with the exception of the gnostics, subscribed to the teachings of historic premillennialism.[12]

Irenaeus (130–202)

Irenaeus was a disciple of Polycarp, who in turn was the disciple of the apostle John. He is known as one of the greatest of the church fathers. Through many of his written works, Irenaeus taught that there will be an appearance of the Antichrist and a period of great tribulation prior to Jesus's second coming. He taught that the church will undergo persecution and that Jesus will return only after the prescribed period of tribulation comes to a close. He actively taught the historic premillennial view, asserting that the returning Lord will establish a millennial kingdom on earth.

Regarding the Antichrist, Irenaeus wrote, "When this Antichrist shall have devastated all things in this world, he will reign for three years and six months, and sit in the temple at Jerusalem; and then the Lord will come from heaven in the clouds, in the glory of the Father, sending this man and those who follow him into the lake of fire."[13] Regarding the church's being caught up in the air to receive the returning Lord, he wrote: "When in the end the church will suddenly be caught up from this, it is said, 'There shall be tribulation such as has not been since the beginning, neither shall be' (Matt 24:21). For this is the last contest of the righteous, in which, when they overcome, they are crowned with

---

11. Justin Martyr, *Dialogue with Trypho* 80, in *ANF* 1:239.
12. Lewis and Demarest, *Integrative Theology*, 3:378.
13. Irenaeus, *Against Heresies* 5.30.4, in *ANF* 1:560.

incorruption."[14] According to Gregg R. Allison, a considerable number of believers in the early church adopted Irenaeus's eschatological view. Irenaeus's doctrine of end times follows this structure: "Christ will return, Antichrist will be defeated, Christians will be resurrected bodily, these believers will reign with Christ on the earth for one thousand years, unbelievers will be resurrected after the millennium, the final judgment will occur and God will establish the eternal state of heaven and hell."[15] In terms of timeline and overall structure, Irenaeus's eschatology coincides with that of historic premillennialism today.

Hippolytus (170–235)

Hippolytus was a church father and theologian who taught and wrote between the end of the second century and the beginning of the third century. He was also a disciple of Irenaeus. He is known to have taught on the eschatological vision of the book of Daniel. He affirmed the appearance of the Antichrist and the ensuing tribulation before the second coming of Jesus. He wrote: "The fourth beast, as being stronger and mightier than all that went before it, will reign five hundred years. When the times are fulfilled, and the ten horns spring from the beast in the last times, then the Antichrist will appear among them. When he makes war against the saints, and persecutes them, then we may expect the manifestation of the Lord from heaven."[16]

In his book *Treatise on Christ and Antichrist*, Hippolytus also wrote: "These things, then, being come to pass, beloved, and the one week being divided into two parts, and the abomination of desolation being manifested then, and the two prophets and forerunners of the Lord having finished their course, and the whole world finally approaching the consummation, what remains but the coming of our Lord and Savior Jesus Christ from

---

14. Irenaeus, *Against Heresies* 5.29.1, in *ANF* 1:558.
15. Allison, *Historical Theology*, 686.
16. Hippolytus, *Fragments from Commentaries* 2.7, in *ANF* 5:179.

heaven, for whom we have looked in hope?"[17] This demonstrates that Hippolytus also embraced the broad eschatological framework of historic premillennialism.

Tertullian (160–225)

One of the most significant Latin church fathers of the late second and early third centuries was Tertullian, who contributed greatly to the formal exposition of the doctrine of the Trinity. Tertullian also advanced the historic premillennial view of eschatology by teaching that Christians will suffer through the great tribulation, that they will be subject to the persecution of the Antichrist, and that their bodies will be transfigured at the time of Jesus's second coming.

> These people also shall, in the crisis of the last moment and from their instantaneous death, while encountering the oppression of Antichrist, undergo a change. They will obtain by this not so much a divestiture of the body as a clothing superimposed upon it with the garment which is from heaven. They shall put on this heavenly garment over their bodies.[18]

Tertullian is known to have taught that those who died in Christ will receive their new resurrection bodies at the time of the second coming.[19]

Concerning the millennial kingdom, Tertullian wrote, "We do confess that a kingdom is promised to us upon the earth, although before heaven, only in another state of existence; insomuch as it will be after the resurrection for a thousand years in the divinely-built city of Jerusalem."[20] Considering his teachings on the timing and nature of the resurrection of the righteous, as well as the location of the millennial kingdom, there is no

---

17. Hippolytus, *Treatise on Christ and Antichrist* 64, in *ANF* 5:218.
18. Tertullian, *Against Marcion* 5.12, in *ANF* 3:455.
19. Tertullian, *Against Marcion* 5.12, in *ANF* 3:455.
20. Tertullian, *Against Marcion* 3.25, in *ANF* 3:342.

doubt that Tertullian also stood behind the historic premillennial framework of biblical eschatology.

Lactantius (240–320)

Lactantius served as the theological advisor of Constantine I, the first Christian Roman emperor, and he also taught Constantine's son as a personal tutor. Based on his extant writings, he advocated the historic premillennial view. "When Christ shall have . . . made the great judgment and restored to life those who were just from the beginning, he will stay among men for a thousand years and will rule them with a most just dominion."[21] In addition, he depicted the millennial kingdom with these vivid descriptions: "Throughout this time beasts shall not be nourished by blood, nor birds by prey; but all things shall be peaceful and tranquil. Lions and calves shall stand together at the manger (hay trough). The wolves shall not carry off the sheep nor the hound wolf (dog) hunt for prey; hawks and eagles shall not injure; the infant shall play with serpents."[22] Here, we can see that Lactantius employed Isaiah 11:6–9 to portray the blessings of the earthly millennial kingdom.

The Latter Part of the Age of the Church Fathers and the Middle Ages (Fourth to Fifteenth Centuries)

The Decline of Historic Premillennialism: Three Reasons

Although it was the dominant view throughout the age of the earliest church fathers, historic premillennialism started to lose ground in the late fourth century AD. According to Allison, three main reasons account for this decline. First is that some church fathers had previously erred by depicting the blessings of the millennium with overly materialistic and extravagant language that alienated the churches. This caused many Christians to perceive

---

21. Lactantius, *Divine Institutes* 24, in *ANF* 7:219.
22. Lactantius, *Divine Institutes* 24, in *ANF* 7:219.

historic premillennialism as a "strange" doctrine. Second, after Constantine I endorsed Christianity as the official religion of the Roman Empire, the relationship between the church and the state changed from that of enmity to that of friendship. With this shift in political dynamics, many believers began to resent and reject the teachings of historic premillennialism, especially those concerning the great tribulation and the persecution of the church. Third, some radical sects attempted to predict, without success, the exact time of Jesus's return and the inauguration of the millennial kingdom. For example, the Montanists advocated what they called the "new prophecy" and stressed the immediacy of Jesus's return. Their radical doomsday predictions added to the church's growing apathy toward historic premillennialism.[23]

The Appearance of the Catechetical School in Alexandria

In addition, new eschatological beliefs and hermeneutical methods grew out of a catechetical school in Alexandria, Egypt, causing historic premillennialism to lose influence in the church. The most notable members of this school were Clement of Alexandria (150–215) and Origen (185–234). Origen is known to have rejected historic premillennialism's literal and historical interpretation of Revelation. Moreover, he popularized the allegorical reading of the Bible, which extracted spiritual and symbolic principles from the Scriptures. As a result, his eschatology rejected literal and historic interpretations of the book of Revelation and gave prominence to the figurative/symbolic interpretation of the written Word.[24]

Tyconius (d. ca. 400) and Augustine (354–430)

Influenced by the teachings of Origen, Tyconius authored a book titled *Libur Regularum* ("The Book of Rules"), in which he proposed seven methods of interpreting the book of Revelation. To

---

23. Allison, *Historical Theology*, 687.
24. Allison, *Historical Theology*, 687.

summarize, these seven methods taught that Revelation is not to be understood in the literal or historic sense, as it had been for the past three centuries, but that its message is to be regarded as representative of spiritual fulfillments in both the church at large and the lives of individual believers. Tyconius therefore proposed an amillennial reading of the book of Revelation. Most importantly, Augustine, who is esteemed as the greatest of the church fathers, was tremendously influenced by Tyconius. For example, Augustine spoke very favorably of Tyconius's *Libur Regularum* in his book *Christian Doctrine*. He also adopted a strong amillennial view in his widely read *The City of God*. For about a thousand years after Augustine's death, amillennialism rose to fame as the dominant eschatological view of the Middle Ages.[25]

The Age of the Reformation
(Sixteenth to Seventeenth Centuries)

Martin Luther (1483–1546) and John Calvin (1509–64)

Martin Luther and John Calvin condemned the corrupt soteriology and ecclesiology of the Roman Catholic Church and successfully restored the apostolic teachings in the Protestant church. However, neither of them challenged the dominant amillennial view of their times. This remains a point of lament regarding the legacy of the Reformers.

Luther taught that Jesus could return at any point, even during his own lifetime. With this firm hope in the second coming, he instructed his students to live with the same eschaton in view. However, he denied the historical and physical reality of the future millennium, resisted the historic premillennial doctrine of eschatology, and remained an amillennialist all his life. Luther viewed the pope of his day as the Antichrist and asserted the need for the Protestant church to overthrow the Roman Catholic Church's demonic powers to establish the true church of Jesus Christ.[26]

25. Allison, *Historical Theology*, 688.
26. Allison, *Historical Theology*, 691.

Seeing some radical Anabaptists' heretical efforts to bring about the new millennium on earth, Calvin strongly opposed the premillennial doctrine of the earthly kingdom. Like Luther, Calvin equated the papacy with the Antichrist and remained an amillennialist all his life.[27] Because of the tremendous authority that Luther and Calvin had, most of the new generations of Reformers and Puritans adopted amillennialism.[28]

Johann Heinrich Alsted (1588–1638) and Joseph Mede (1586–1638)

But there were some exceptions. During the Reformation, two theologians made attempts to restore historic premillennialism to its prominent place in biblical theology. One was Johann Heinrich Alsted and the other was Joseph Mede.

Alsted was a German Calvinist scholar trained under Johannes Piscator (1546–1625), a Reformed theologian in Heidelberg. As a logician, encyclopedist, and also a theologian in the latter part of his life, Alsted defended orthodox trinitarianism from the attacks of anti-trinitarians and unitarians.[29] Moreover, he openly advocated for millenarianism in his book *The Beloved City*. Referencing Old Testament prophetic texts such as Isaiah 2:1–4 and 34:1–17, Alsted provided a detailed commentary on the future reality of the earthly millennium. In this book, he also identified the millennium as an age of peace on earth after all the enemies of God have been destroyed.[30]

Joseph Mede, by contrast, was an English scholar who studied at Cambridge University.[31] He popularized Alsted's historic premillennialism via his influential book *The Key to the Revelation*. Mede understood the history of humanity as consisting of

---

27. Allison, *Historical Theology*, 691.
28. Allison, *Historical Theology*, 691.
29. Wikipedia, s.v. "Johann Heinrich Alsted."
30. Allison, *Historical Theology*, 692.
31. Wikipedia, s.v. "Joseph Mede."

three ages, the last age corresponding to the eschaton of the book of Revelation. He believed that in the battle of Armageddon, the Antichrist—interpreted, again, as the Roman Catholic papacy—will be destroyed. He also believed that Jesus Christ will return at that point and that the earthly millennium will be established soon thereafter.[32] Allison comments that the works of Alsted and Mede helped to revive historic premillennialism as a prominent eschatological view within the Protestant movement.[33]

Historic Premillennialism and Puritan Theologians

Several Puritan theologians who participated in the production of the Westminster Confession of Faith also espoused historic premillennialism. One of the representative figures is Thomas Goodwin (1600–1680), a renowned English Puritan theologian.[34] He studied at Cambridge University, ministered as chaplain to Oliver Cromwell, and served as President of Magdalen College of Oxford University.[35] A considerable number of Puritans and their descendants who immigrated to New England in the new world also held to the historic premillennial view. These included John Davenport (1597–1670), Samuel Mather (1626–71), Increase Mather (1639–1723), Cotton Mather (1663–1728), Samuel Sewall (1652–1730), and Timothy Dwight (1752–1817).[36] This evidence challenges the common assumption among theologians today that all the Puritans who immigrated to America were amillennialists. While it is true that many influential Protestant Reformers espoused the amillennial view, we should not forget that there was also a notable historic premillennial presence in their midst.

---

32. Allison, *Historical Theology*, 692.
33. Allison, *Historical Theology*, 692.
34. Montgomery, "Millennium," 359.
35. *Wikipedia*, s.v. "Thomas Goodwin."
36. Montgomery, "Millennium," 359.

The Church in the Modern Age
(Eighteenth to Nineteenth Centuries)

There were several prominent theologians and commentators who held to the historic premillennial view in the eighteenth and nineteenth centuries. They include: Joseph Priestly (1733–1804), Reformed Baptist theologian of England John Gill (1697–1771), British commentator Henry Alford (1810–71), British commentator Charles Ellicott (1819–1905), Anglican bishop and supporter of evangelicalism J. C. Ryle (1816–1900), British Particular Baptist preacher and Calvinist thinker Charles H. Spurgeon (1834–92), British evangelist Benjamin Willis Newton (1807–99), German Lutheran commentator Franz Delitzsch (1813–90), German Lutheran scholar Theodor Zahn (1838–1933), and German Calvinist commentator Peter Lange (1802–84).[37]

Henry Drummond (1851–97)

Historic premillennialism was restored as a prominent eschatological view of the church by the works of Alsted and Mede in the seventeenth century. It was accepted by some Puritan theologians and, finally, in the early part of the nineteenth century, it gained the support of the church at large through the Albury Conferences of 1826–30, which were spearheaded by Henry Drummond.[38] According to Allison, Drummond devised his own unique bent on premillennialism. He is known to have taught a great divine judgment on the church and a Jewish return to the promised land, both before the second coming of Jesus. After all of this, Drummond argued, the earthly millennial kingdom will be established on earth. Through Drummond's work, historic premillennialism gained favor in every denomination of the Protestant movement.[39]

---

37. Lewis and Demarest, *Integrative Theology*, 3:378.
38. Couch, ed., *Dictionary of Premillennial Theology*, 36.
39. Allison, *Historical Theology*, 693.

The Appearance of Dispensationalism

In the middle of the nineteenth century, historic premillennialism faced a whole different challenge. This was because Britain's John Nelson Darby (1800–1882) put forth a new view known as dispensational premillennialism. According to Darby, God has different purposes for Israel and the church in redemptive history. Not only do Israel and the gentile church have *discrete destinies and hopes*, the church will be raptured by Jesus *before* the great tribulation while the Jews will undergo Antichrist's persecution. After having been raptured and having participated in the feast of the lamb, the church, with Christ, will return to earth. Then Christ will establish the millennium and will also restore the Jewish temple and the priesthood of Israel.

The Spread of Dispensationalism

Dispensational premillennialism grew out of nineteenth-century England, but it had the greatest influence in nineteenth- and twentieth-century America. One important representative proponent of this new view was Dwight L. Moody (1837–99). He contributed to the spreading of dispensationalism by introducing it to the Niagara Bible Conferences. Following Moody, William Blackstone (1841–1935), the author of *Jesus Is Coming*, strongly defended the dispensational view. Blackstone's contemporary, C. I. Scofield (1843–1921), also defended this view in the *Scofield Reference Bible* of 1909. Lewis Sperry Chafer (1871–1952), who founded and served as the first president of Dallas Theological Seminary, forcefully defended dispensationalism as well in his *Systematic Theology*. Dispensationalism, however, truly rose to its present standing of fame and prestige through popular literature like Hal Lindsey's *The Late Great Planet Earth* and Tim LaHaye and Jerry B. Jenkins's *Left Behind* series.

Historic Premillennialism in Western Evangelical Theology Today (Twentieth to Twenty-First Centuries)

Charles Erdman (1866–1960) and Historic Premillennialism

While dispensationalism gained popular support among the general public, historic premillennialism started to gain wide support and attention among theologically trained evangelicals. One of the twentieth-century champions of historic premillennialism was Charles Erdman, who as an American Presbyterian pastor and a professor of theology at Princeton Theological Seminary. He contributed greatly to the spread of historic premillennialism. In his commentary *The Revelation of John: An Exposition* (1936), he interpreted the message of Revelation from a markedly historic premillennial position.

George E. Ladd (1911–82) and the Revival of Historic Premillennialism

George E. Ladd was the most notable proponent of historic premillennialism in the twentieth century. He received his doctorate degree from Harvard University and taught at Fuller Theological Seminary as a New Testament scholar. He advanced the historic premillennial view through well-known works like *The Gospel of the Kingdom* (1959), *The Last Things* (1978), *A Theology of the New Testament* (1993), and *A Commentary on the Revelation of John* (1972). Ladd specifically taught that the first coming of Jesus had inaugurated the kingdom of God, but that this kingdom is still in a state of incompletion. It is his view that God's call upon Christians is for them to live in this age of tension as they work out their salvation in hopes of the promised end. Ladd's interpretation is characteristic of a moderately futuristic perspective rather than a thoroughly futurist perspective. Many evangelical biblical scholars and systematic theologians have been influenced by Ladd's work and, as a result, have adopted historic premillennialism as the most biblically sound teaching on the doctrine of eschatology.

Historic Premillennialism in the Western Evangelical Movement

Biblical Theologians Espousing Historic Premillennialism

Robert H. Gundry (b. 1932)

Robert H. Gundry received his doctorate degree from Manchester University in England and served as a New Testament professor for nearly forty years at Westmont College in California. He persuasively wrote in *The Church and the Tribulation: A Biblical Examination of Posttribulationism* (1973) that the church will not be raptured before the great tribulation but that it will suffer through the prophesied trials and be raptured only at the time of Jesus's second coming. In another work, *First the Antichrist: Why Christ Won't Come before the Antichrist Does* (1977), Gundry voiced the historic premillennial view that the Antichrist will make his appearance before the second coming of Jesus and will rule over the whole world with violence and persecution. Gundry is widely accepted as an authority on Matthew's Gospel within the Western evangelical community.

D. A. Carson (b. 1946)

D. A. Carson is internationally acclaimed as an authority on the New Testament. Born in Canada, he completed his doctorate degree at Cambridge University and then went on to Trinity Evangelical Divinity School in Chicago to serve as a professor of New Testament (1978–). Carson has never written a complete book or journal article on historic premillennialism. However, he openly admits that he holds to the historic premillennial view and has always given support to the historic premillennial doctrine of eschatology. According to Craig Blomberg, a former student of his, Carson adheres closely to the views of historic premillennialism.

Douglas J. Moo (b. 1950)

Douglas J. Moo is an authority on Pauline theology and the general epistles of the New Testament. He received his doctorate from the University of Saint Andrews in Scotland and served as a New Testament professor at Trinity Evangelical Divinity School for over twenty years. In 2000, he moved to Wheaton College, where he continued to serve as a distinguished professor of New Testament. He authored commentaries on Romans, Colossians, Philemon, James, 1–2 Peter, and Jude and also contributed a chapter, titled "A Case for the Posttribulation Rapture,"[40] in the recently published *Three Views on the Rapture* (2010).[41] Here, Moo provides Scripture-based criticism of the pretribulation rapture theory and successfully demonstrates that a posttribulation rapture is the more biblical of these eschatological timelines. In his promotion of the posttribulation rapture theory, Moo argues that historic premillennialism is also the most biblical view of eschatology.

Craig L. Blomberg (b. 1955)

Craig L. Blomberg is an internationally renowned New Testament scholar who holds to the historic premillennial view. Blomberg received his doctorate degree at Aberdeen University in England under the guidance of I. Howard Marshall. Since 1986, he has served at Denver Seminary as Professor of New Testament. In various written works, Blomberg has clarified that in his view historic premillennialism is the most biblical of the eschatological views. A representative work of his is *From Pentecost to Patmos: An Introduction to Acts through Revelation* (2006), in which he acknowledges the different views on the millennium and identifies himself with the historic premillennial camp.[42] Here, Blomberg discusses the relationship between the great tribulation and the rapture and seeks to demonstrate biblically that Jesus will return to earth at the

---

40. Moo, "Case for the Posttribulation Rapture," 185–241.
41. Gundry, ed., *Three Views on the Rapture*.
42. Gundry, ed., *Three Views on the Rapture*, 518.

end of the prophesied tribulation. Blomberg is also a proponent of the historic premillennial view that Christians will be caught up in the air to greet the returning Lord and then come back down to earth to partake in the blessings of the earthly millennium.[43]

Blomberg also argues that futurism is a better hermeneutical approach to Revelation than idealism, preterism, and historicism.[44] Thus, it should be interpreted as referring to the yet-to-come last days and not as depicting events in the first century (preterism) or throughout the whole of church history (idealism).

In 2007, Denver Seminary hosted a Biblical Studies Conference on historic premillennialism. Here, Blomberg presented a paper titled "The Posttribulationism of the New Testament: Leaving 'Left Behind' Behind." In this paper, Blomberg successfully argued against dispensational pretribulationism/rapturism from the historic premillennial view. In 2009, the same seminary hosted an international conference of historic premillennialism.[45] Blomberg spoke three times at this conference as a keynote speaker and defended historic premillennialism as a more biblical and faithful interpretation than dispensationalism or amillennialism. The titles of his influential lectures are: "Why We Don't Have to Wait for the Great Commission to Be Fulfilled before Christ Returns: The Problems with Postmillennialism," "The Need for a Millennium beyond the Present Age: The Anticlimax of Amillennialism," and "Inappropriately Privileging Israel: Why Historic Premillennialism Trumps Dispensationalism."

Other Biblical Scholars

Apart from the biblical scholars mentioned above, there are many others who hold to the historic premillennial view. For example, Robert H. Mounce (b. 1921), President Emeritus of Whitworth University in Spokane, Washington, is a proponent of historic

---

43. Gundry, ed., *Three Views on the Rapture*, 518.
44. Gundry, ed., *Three Views on the Rapture*, 518–19.
45. At this conference, I presented a paper entitled "Who Are the Two Witnesses in Revelation 11? An Integration of Western and Asian Proposals."

MODELS OF PREMILLENNIALISM

premillennialism. In his commentary *The Book of Revelation*, he shared his conviction that historic premillennialism is the most biblical view of the end times.

Grant R. Osborne (b. 1942), long-time Professor of New Testament at Trinity Evangelical Divinity School, also takes the futurist approach that coincides with the basic framework of historic premillennialism. His commentary on Revelation demonstrates his clear historic premillennial disposition.[46]

Craig S. Keener (b. 1960), currently F. M. and Ada Thompson Professor of Biblical Studies at Asbury Theological Seminary, is another prominent historic premillennial biblical scholar. He received his doctorate degree from Duke University and served as a professor at Palmer Theological Seminary until he relocated to Asbury in 2011. In his commentary on Revelation,[47] Keener argues that historic premillennialism is the eschatological system most consistent with the overarching themes and teachings of the Bible.

George R. Beasley-Murray (1916–2000) is another voice representing historic premillennialism. He was a British biblical scholar who served as Principal of Spurgeon's College in London and later took office as James Buchanan Harrison Professor of New Testament at Southern Baptist Theological Seminary. In his commentary *The Book of Revelation*, Beasley-Murray adopted the historic premillennial position on biblical eschatology. In his book *Jesus and the Last Days*, he also interpreted the Olivet Discourse in Matthew 13 from a uniquely historic premillennial lens.[48]

Richard S. Hess (b. 1954), an internationally renowned Old Testament scholar, also espouses the historic premillennial doctrine of eschatology. Hess currently holds office as the Distinguished Professor of Old Testament at Denver Seminary. At the 2007 Denver Seminary Biblical Studies Conference, he presented a paper titled "The Future Written in the Past: The Old Testament and the Millennium."[49] Here, Hess argued that the prophecy of

---

46. Osborne, *Revelation*.
47. Keener, *Revelation*.
48. Beasley-Murray, *Jesus and the Last Days*.
49. Hess, "Future Written in the Past," 23–36.

the earthly millennium is first found in the Old Testament prophets. In 2009, Hess presented another paper titled "The Seventy Sevens of Daniel 9: A Timetable for the Future?," defending the historic premillennial view from the criticisms of both amillennialism and dispensationalism.

Ben Witherington III (b. 1951) is yet another internationally renowned New Testament scholar who is committed to the teachings of historic premillennialism. He holds office as the Jean R. Amos Professor of New Testament for Doctoral Studies at Asbury Theological Seminary. In his work *Jesus, Paul, and the End of the World: A Comparative Study in New Testament Eschatology*, Witherington advocates for and strengthens the eschatological vision of historic premillennialism. He also authored a book titled *Revelation*, which relays the historic premillennial interpretation of the book of Revelation.

M. Daniel Carroll Rodas (b. 19), currently Blanchard Professor of Old Testament at Wheaton College Graduate School, is internationally renowned in the field of Old Testament ethics. He also holds to the historic premillennial doctrine of the end times. He especially notices that there is a clear resonance between the biblical view of social justice and historic premillennialism's teaching on the millennial kingdom. Carroll has repeatedly articulated this point through his teachings and writings.[50]

Systematic Theologians Espousing Historic Premillennialism

Millard J. Erickson (b. 1932)

Millard J. Erickson is a renowned American evangelical systematic theologian within the Reformed Baptist tradition. In his acclaimed book *Christian Theology*, now in its third edition, Erickson has identified historic premillennialism as the view that is most harmonious with the message of the Bible as a whole.[51] He also believes that posttribulationism is much more compatible

---

50. As reported in personal conversations with the present author.
51. Erickson, *Christian Theology*, 1222–24.

with Christian doctrine.⁵² Erickson clearly identifies himself as a historic premillennialist and further expounds his historic premillennial convictions in a book titled *A Basic Guide to Eschatology: Making Sense of the Millennium*.

Wayne A. Grudem (b. 1948)

Wayne A. Grudem is yet another Reformed Baptist theologian who holds to the historic premillennial view. After graduating from Harvard University, Grudem continued his studies at Westminster Theological Seminary and received his doctorate degree at Cambridge University in England. For about twenty years, Grudem served as Professor of Systematic Theology at Trinity Evangelical Divinity School in Chicago and he has been teaching systematic theology at Phoenix Seminary since 2001. In his book *Systematic Theology*, Grudem avers that historic premillennialism is the most biblically sound teaching on the doctrine of the end times.

Bruce A. Demarest (b. 1935)

Bruce A. Demarest is a Reformed theologian within the American evangelical Presbyterian tradition. He taught systematic theology and spiritual formation at Denver Seminary for over thirty years until his recent retirement in 2011. He co-authored *Integrative Theology* with Gordon R. Lewis (1926–2016). This book presented historic premillennialism as the most biblical view of end-time prophecies. Because Lewis was a dispensationalist, the book does not treat historic premillennialism in detail. Nevertheless, Demarest remained committed to the historic premillennial view. In 2009, he participated in the Denver Seminary Biblical Studies Conference and presented a paper titled "What Did the Early Church Believe about the Tribulation?" With this paper, he demonstrated that the early church and most of the church fathers held to historic premillennialism, believing that the church will

---

52. Erickson, *Christian Theology*, 1230–31.

experience the designated time of tribulation, participate in a posttribulation rapture at the time of Jesus's second coming, and rule with Christ in the earthly millennial kingdom.

Conclusion

Many models of premillennialism have been held throughout church history. My conviction is that among these models, historic premillennialism represents the most faithful interpretation of biblical eschatology. This, of course, is not to say that the other views are heretical, or that those who adhere to them are in danger of falling from the grace of God. Each of the other views has something important to add to the biblical doctrine of eschatology. This being the case, I do not find it fitting to condemn the other views. Instead, I propose that constructive aspects of these other views be actively incorporated into the overarching system of historic premillennialism. The reason I perceive historic premillennialism to be the best-fitting framework of biblical eschatology is because, despite some of its weaknesses, and despite some of the strengths other views display, historic premillennialism at large proves to be the most hermeneutically responsible and integrated doctrine of biblical eschatology. Today, historic premillennialism is gaining ground among evangelical communities around the world. Especially in the West, we see that many of the most influential evangelical biblical scholars and systematic theologians are strong advocates of historic premillennialism. Similarly, historic premillennialism is finding many followers in Korea, Singapore, and other Asian countries.

Of course, dispensationalism continues to find support from the general public, but it is quickly becoming an outdated view among professionally trained theologians. This decline led to internal conflict among dispensational scholars. Recently, we have seen the development of progressive dispensationalism, which is somewhat similar to historic premillennialism.

Ultimately, the single most important point I want to emphasize in this chapter is that future theological discussions relating to eschatology must cease to be contentious. Fractious arguments are a terrible waste of our theological resources. Instead, I suggest that scholars and theologians work together to flesh out the biblical doctrine of eschatology and consider afresh the ancient framework of historic premillennialism. Given that Jesus's return is quickly drawing near, we must not allow a spirit of contention to dominate our future discussions. It is only through sound biblical hermeneutics and the integration of truly biblical views that we are able to fulfill our duties as the teachers and servants of Jesus's bride, the church.

In the past, controversial debates regarding Jesus's divinity and the triune nature of the Godhead were put to rest by humble theologians who integrated various views within the large framework of the Nicene Creed, formulated by the Council of Nicaea in AD 325. The same is true of the doctrine of justification, which united the views of evangelical Reformers during the Reformation. Indeed, in my opinion, the time has come for evangelical theologians to reconsider doctrinal unity within the large framework of historic premillennialism, with its ancient pedigree and its claim to be the most biblical doctrine of eschatology. Consider the fact that it was only when the doctrine of the Trinity was agreed upon by theologians that churches were able to fight against numerous heretical teachings regarding the nature of God. The same is true of the doctrine of justification. For it was when the Reformers collaborated to establish the united evangelical position on this point of debate that they were able to refute the unbiblical practices and theological errors that plagued the Catholic Church. The present discussion of eschatology is no different. Evangelical churches would benefit from agreement about the large framework of biblical eschatology in order to defend the church from the many erroneous teachings concerning the end times. Surely, this is part and parcel of the high calling God has given us as we prepare for and hope in the glorious second coming of Jesus Christ.

Those scholars who agree that historic premillennialism is the most biblical view that frames the Bible's doctrine of eschatology will need to further engage the task of refining the details of the historic premillennial view to make it more biblically sound—free of interpretive dilemmas and communicable to local churches and individual believers. Of course, no doctrine or interpretation can be flawless in the sense that God and the Bible are flawless. However, it still remains that proponents of historic premillennialism need to diligently engage the refining work that makes it more biblical and more intelligible. This, I believe, is the new horizon of theological research concerning the global evangelical community's inquiry into the study of biblical eschatology and the book of Revelation.

2

Classical Dispensational Premillennialism

—Sung Wook Chung

Introduction

IN THIS CHAPTER WE will examine classical dispensational premillennialism, focusing on its hermeneutical principles, major tenets, and origins, as well as its development throughout the history of Western and global Christianity. Classical dispensational premillennialism is a view with vigorous advocates, a profound legacy, and a tremendous tradition within the church. It is certainly not an overstatement to conclude that many Bible-believing, fundamentalist, and conservative evangelical Christians today also hold to the classical dispensational premillennial view, especially in the North American context.

Without a doubt, classical dispensational premillennialism has dominated the field of eschatology for the past two centuries or so. Gaining momentum in the United States, this view secured remarkable support through the publication of popular books and other forms of media. The most notable recent title is Jerry B. Jenkins and Tim LaHaye's *Left Behind* series.[1] *Left Behind* is a sixteen-volume fictional series that sold millions of copies in the United States alone and has been adapted into a motion picture and other spin-offs, amplifying its already huge impact on the masses. At any

---

1. LaHaye and Jenkins, *Left Behind Series*.

rate, the point worth mentioning here is that most of the people who have been influenced by the classical dispensational view have not been trained scholars, but rather the general public. Today, dispensationalism has a prominent influence in the Bible Belt of the American southeast. There, we find many Christian schools that teach dispensational premillennialist convictions.

Hermeneutical Principles and Fundamental Tenets

Dispensations and the Privileges of the Jews

One of the most fundamental hermeneutical principles of classical dispensational premillennialism is related to dividing God's economy of redemption into several "dispensations" or "ages," during which God demonstrates special ways of administering the world and saving humanity. According to typical classical dispensationalism, there are seven dispensations: innocence (Adam before the fall), conscience (from the fall to the great flood), human government (from the great flood to the tower of Babel), promise (from Abraham to Moses), the law (from Moses to Jesus), grace (from Jesus to the rapture of the church), and the millennium (a thousand-year reign of Christ on earth).

In this system, different dispensations have different ways of salvation. For instance, in the dispensation of the law, humans are saved by keeping the law, whereas in the dispensation of grace, humans are saved by grace through faith apart from the works of the law. As we will argue in later chapters, progressive dispensationalism objects to this idea of multiple ways of salvation and demonstrates that there is only one way of salvation, which is through faith, by grace, and in Jesus Christ alone.

Another fundamental hermeneutical principle of classical dispensational premillennialism is a rather sharp distinction between the Jews and the gentile church that privileges the former. According to the typical dispensational scheme, the Jews are the primary people of God while the gentile church is the people of God in a secondary and subsidiary sense. Classical dispensational premillennialists believe that the Jews are specially elected to enjoy the privileged status over the gentile church throughout God's economy of redemption, including the age of the church and the millennium. As a corollary, God's promises given to the Jews in the Old Testament must be fulfilled literally in and through the offspring of the physical Jews, not in and through the church, "spiritual Israel." For example, God's promises in relation to the land in the context of the covenant with Abraham must be fulfilled literally by the Jews' inheriting the Palestinian land someday in the future.

On the basis of these presuppositions, classical dispensational premillennialism rejects replacement theology,[2] or supersessionism,[3] which teaches that the church has completely replaced Israel as the people of God because the Old Testament promises to the ethnic Jews were fulfilled in and through the church, the new and true Israel. In stark contrast, classical dispensational premillennialism continues to privilege ethnic Jews over the church, which is primarily composed of gentiles.

Literal and Futurist Interpretation of Revelation 20:1–6

Another significant hermeneutical principle of classical dispensational premillennialism is the literal and futurist interpretation of biblical prophecies in general and Revelation 20 in particular, which describes the millennial kingdom. This is closely connected with the rejection of a symbolic and spiritual reading of Revelation 20, which has been a dominant interpretative paradigm in both amillennialist and postmillennialist circles. In contrast, this is an important commonality between historic premillennialism and classical dispensational premillennialism. Revelation 20:1–3 tells us that Satan will be completely bound into the abyss for a thousand years. Satan will be kept from deceiving the nations

---

2. For an excellent dispensational critique of replacement theology, see Vlach, *Has the Church Replaced Israel?*

3. See Vlach, *Church as a Replacement of Israel.*

until the thousand years end. After the thousand years, Satan must be released for a short time.

In addition, Revelation 20:4–6 tells us that those who have been given authority to judge will be seated on thrones. Those who have been beheaded and have not worshiped the beast or its image will come to life and reign with Christ a thousand years. There are still scholarly debates and disputes over who these people are. Many historic premillennial scholars argue that these will be all true Christians, including martyrs, or alternatively they will be martyrs alone who have been killed not only throughout church history but also during the great tribulation right before the parousia. In contrast, classical dispensational premillennialists tend to argue that those who will be given authority to judge and reign will be *the Jews* rather than the gentiles. Of course, this is a debatable point between historic premillennialists and classical dispensational premillennialists.

Nevertheless, from the perspective of a literal, futurist interpretation of this passage, it is crystal clear that whoever they may be, those who will experience the first resurrection will reign with Christ for a thousand years. The second death will have no power over them and they will be priests of God and of Christ.

For classical dispensational premillennialists, Revelation 20:1–6 must be interpreted literally, not symbolically or spiritually, as most amillennialists and postmillennialists have been interpreting it. Moreover, this passage must be interpreted from the futurist, not preterist,[4] perspective. For example, most amillennialists interpret this passage symbolically and spiritually, arguing that the binding of Satan is symbolic of the defeat of Satan that already happened when Jesus Christ was crucified for our sin and was resurrected from the dead for our righteousness. Classical dispensational premillennialists view the symbolic and preterist interpretation of the passage to be groundless because

---

4. The preterist perspective is a way to approach Revelation, which presupposes that Revelation 6–19 depicts events that have already been fulfilled, either during John's lifetime or by the time of the destruction of Jerusalem in AD 70.

the devil is still prowling "around like a roaring lion looking for someone to devour" (1 Pet 5:8). According to 1 Peter 5:8, Satan seems not completely bound but rather still very active in devouring and deceiving people.

Therefore, there are significant commonalities between classical dispensational premillennialism and historic premillennialism in terms of hermeneutical principles, despite major differences in terms of the interpretation of the timing of the rapture and the character of the millennial kingdom.

Chronological Interpretation of Revelation 19–20

For classical dispensational premillennialists, the literal, futurist interpretation of Revelation 20:1–6 is closely connected with the chronological interpretation of Revelation 19–20. Most interpreters of the book of Revelation, including those committed to classical dispensational premillennialism, concur that Revelation 19 talks about the second coming of the Lord Jesus Christ. In particular, Revelation 19:19–21 tells us that both the beast and the false prophet will be captured and thrown alive into the fiery lake of burning sulfur. So two members of the evil trinity, not including Satan, have already been thrown into the lake of fire by chapter 20.

After the depiction of the Lord's second coming in Revelation 19, Revelation 20:1–6 describes the millennial reign of Christ and his saints. According to 20:7–10, after the millennial kingdom, Satan will be released for a short time and go out to deceive the nations in the four corners of the earth. Many will be deceived and will participate in Satan's attempt to attack the city of God's people. But they will be devoured by the fire from heaven. And then the devil will be "thrown into the lake of burning sulfur, where the beast and the false prophet had been thrown" (v. 10). This is the description of the final destiny of Satan. It is very important to note here that when the devil was thrown to the lake of fire, he found the beast and the false prophet there, who had already been thrown in before him.[5]

---

5. For an excellent exposition in line with the present authors' arguments, see Blomberg, "Posttribulationism of the New Testament," 61–88.

This strongly implies that there is a chronological order among these three crucial eschatological events, namely, the parousia of Revelation 19, the millennium of Revelation 20:1–6, and Satan's final judgment of Revelation 20:7–10.

Pretribulational Rapture: The Church Escapes from the Great Tribulation

Most classical dispensational premillennialists advocate a *pre*tribulational rapture rather than a *post*tribulational rapture.[6] This means that there will be a period of "great tribulation" (Greek, *thlipsis megas*) before the parousia and that the church will escape from this tribulation by being suddenly raptured, contra what historic premillennialism contends. This is the critical and crucial discrepancy between historic premillennialism and classical dispensational premillennialism.

Classical dispensational premillennialism appeals to Daniel 9:24–27 to legitimize its advocacy of a seven-year tribulation. There, a mysterious figure named Gabriel relates the following vision:

> Seventy "sevens" are decreed for your people and your holy city to finish transgression, to put an end to sin, to atone for wickedness, to bring in everlasting righteousness, to seal up vision and prophecy and to anoint the Most Holy Place.
>
> Know and understand this: From the time the word goes out to restore and rebuild Jerusalem until the Anointed One, the ruler, comes, there will be seven "sevens," and sixty-two "sevens." It will be rebuilt with streets and a trench, but in times of trouble. After the sixty-two "sevens," the Anointed One will be put to death and will have nothing. The people of the ruler who will come will destroy the city and the sanctuary. The end will come like a flood: War will continue until the end, and desolations

---

6. See Walvoord, *Rapture Question*; Feinberg, "Case for the Pretribulation Rapture Position," 45–86; Lewis and Demarest, *Integrative Theology*, 3:369–444.

have been decreed. He will confirm a covenant with many for one "seven." In the middle of the "seven" he will put an end to sacrifice and offering. And at the temple he will set up an abomination that causes desolation, until the end that is decreed is poured out on him.

Classical dispensational premillennialists believe that the idea of seventy "sevens" provides a distinct way of understanding God's eschatological dealings with not only the history of Israel but also redemptive history as a whole. The last "seven" in the above passage, according to most classical dispensational pre-millennialists, indicates the final seven years of great tribulation right after the rapture of the church. The Antichrist will confirm a covenant with humanity for a period of seven years, in the middle of which he "will set up an abomination that causes desolation" (v. 27). When Jesus Christ refers to "the abomination that causes desolation" in Matthew 24:15, classical dispensational premillennialists believe that Jesus is mentioning the rise of the Antichrist and his subsequent persecution of the Jews after the sudden rapture of the church.

In addition, classical dispensational premillennialists present a variety of biblical passages as evidence for a pretribulational rapture. For example, 1 Thessalonians 1:10 states, "and to wait for his Son from heaven, whom he raised from the dead—Jesus, who rescues us from the coming wrath." Classical dispensational premillennialists construe "the coming wrath" not as the final judgment upon sinners but rather the great tribulation. Thus, they believe that Jesus Christ will rescue the church from the great tribulation. In 1 Thessalonians 4:13–18, Paul states:

> Brothers and sisters, we do not want you to be uninformed about those who sleep in death, so that you do not grieve like the rest of mankind, who have no hope. For we believe that Jesus died and rose again, and so we believe that God will bring with Jesus those who have fallen asleep in him. According to the Lord's word, we tell you that we who are still alive, who are left until the coming of the Lord, will certainly not precede those who have fallen asleep. For the Lord himself will come down from heaven, with a loud command, with the

voice of the archangel and with the trumpet call of God, and the dead in Christ will rise first. After that, we who are still alive and are left will be caught up together with them in the clouds to meet the Lord in the air. And so we will be with the Lord forever. Therefore encourage one another with these words.

According to classical dispensationalists, the event of believers being caught up together in the clouds to meet with the Lord in the air will happen before the great tribulation. For them, this event is not about the parousia after the great tribulation, as historic premillennialists have been arguing, but it is rather about Christ's secret coming in the sky and welcoming the church to the sky. After the rapture of the church, the church will enjoy a wedding feast with the Lord Jesus Christ, while the Jews and non-believing gentiles suffer the great tribulation characterized by the Antichrist's violent dictatorship and three series of plagues: seven seals, seven trumpets, and seven bowls. This entails that for classical dispensational premillennialists, we will have not one second coming of Jesus Christ but rather *two*—one of which is secret and the other public.

First Thessalonians 5:9 says, "For God did not appoint us to suffer wrath but to receive salvation through our Lord Jesus Christ." Dispensational premillennialists interpret this verse to mean that God will not allow believers to suffer wrath—i.e., the great tribulation—but they will receive salvation—namely, rapture before the great tribulation. Revelation 4:1 states, "After this I looked, and there before me was a door standing open in heaven. And the voice I had first heard speaking to me like a trumpet said, 'Come up here, and I will show you what must take place after this.'" Many dispensational premillennialists interpret the phrase "come up here" to be indicating God's command for the church to be raptured. Thus, after the church is lifted up, both nonbelievers and the Jews are left behind and suffer the great tribulation, during which the Antichrist reigns with terror.

The most powerful example of the interpretive differences between the classical dispensational premillennialist view and that of historic premillennialism is Revelation 13:10, which states, "If anyone is to go into captivity, into captivity they will go. If anyone is to be killed with the sword, with the sword they will be killed. This calls for patient endurance and faithfulness on the part of God's people." This passage teaches clearly, from a historic premillennial perspective, that God's people—that is, the church—should endure the tribulation with patience and faithfulness. However, in stark contrast, classical dispensationalists interpret "God's people" here to be the Jews left behind after the church's rapture. It is important, however, to note in this context that the book of Revelation is given not for the Jews but for the churches, as Revelation 22:16 states: "I, Jesus, have sent my angel to give you this testimony *for the churches*. I am the Root and the Offspring of David, and the bright Morning Star." Thus, "God's people" in chapter 13 should arguably be construed to be churches rather than the Jews.

Three Resurrections

Classical dispensational premillennialists believe that there will be three resurrections of humanity. The first resurrection will occur when the Lord comes again secretly to rapture the church before the great tribulation. The deceased saints will be resurrected then. The second resurrection will occur when the Lord comes again publicly, after the great tribulation, in order to establish the earthly millennial kingdom. Only the saints who died during the great tribulation, primarily the Jewish martyrs, will be resurrected. The third resurrection will occur at the end of the millennium before the judgment at the great white throne. All unbelievers will be raised again for final judgment.

From both amillennialist and postmillennialist perspectives, the idea of three resurrections appears to be too complex. Even historic premillennialists who advocate two end-time resurrections disagree with the classical dispensational premillennialist claim that there will be three resurrections. However, classical dispensationalists are convinced of such an interpretation.

Millennial Kingdom on Earth: Penultimate State

Most classical dispensational premillennialists argue that the millennial kingdom will be established on earth as the penultimate state of the world before the consummation of the kingdom, the coming of the eternal new heaven and new earth. The rationale for such an interpretation is that the physical, spatio-temporal paradise must be restored to the present, existing world before the dawn of the eternalized and glorified cosmos, which Scripture calls "the new heaven and the new earth."

Who will reign with Christ in the millennial kingdom? The responses to this question by classical dispensational premillennialists are considerably different from those of historic premillennialists. According to historic premillennialism, the resurrected saints, including not only Jewish believers but also gentile Christians, will reign with Christ in the millennial kingdom.[7] But for classical dispensational premillennialists, only the resurrected Jews or Jewish martyrs will reign with Christ in the millennial kingdom. Thus, the millennial kingdom will exhibit a peculiar Jewish flavor. In addition, many classical dispensational premillennialists believe that the Jewish temple will be rebuilt in the millennial kingdom and that even the Jewish priestly system will be restored. As we have seen, the rationale behind these arguments is that God grants the Jews spiritual privileges over the gentiles throughout redemptive history and that God's prophecies and promises given to the Old Testament Jews should be fulfilled literally.

Critical Engagement

There are several major difficulties with classical dispensational premillennialism. One of the most significant difficulties is its two-tiered hermeneutical scheme, distinguishing God's redemptive dealings with the Jews and with the gentiles rather sharply

---

7. Of course, there are minority views on this issue among historic premillennialists. For example, Robert H. Mounce argues that only martyrs will reign with Christ in the millennium. See Mounce, *Book of Revelation*, 345–78.

and privileging the Jews over the gentiles. However, the New Testament in general and the Pauline epistles in particular do not support this hermeneutical framework. For example, Paul writes in Ephesians 2:14–18 as follows:

> For he [Christ] himself is our peace, who has made the two groups [Jews and the nations] one and has destroyed the barrier, the dividing wall of hostility, by setting aside in his flesh the law with its commands and regulations. His purpose was to create in himself one new humanity out of the two, thus making peace, and in one body to reconcile both of them to God through the cross, by which he put to death their hostility. He came and preached peace to you who were far away and peace to those who were near. For through him we both have access to the Father by one Spirit.

According to this passage, God creates "one new humanity" in Jesus Christ, reconciling and combining Jews and gentiles with each other. This one new humanity is "a new kind of man," totally different from the current humanity, as C. S. Lewis has argued.[8] Therefore, "There is neither Jew nor gentile, neither slave nor free, nor is there male and female, for you are all one in Christ Jesus" (Gal 3:28). Though it is still debatable whether the church completely has replaced Israel,[9] it seems untenable that God's favor has always been upon the Jews, making the gentiles a subsidiary factor in God's redemptive history.

Another major difficulty with classical dispensational premillennialism is its rather peculiar view of Israel. As a matter of fact, this issue is closely connected with its hermeneutical scheme. Many classical dispensational premillennialists believe that the national state of Israel must be reestablished in the last days, so that Old Testament prophecies and promises in relation to Israel may be fulfilled literally—especially the promise concerning the land of Israel. Furthermore, they contend that the

---

8. Lewis, *Mere Christianity*, 62.

9. For an excellent discussion on replacement theology from an appreciative perspective, see Diprose, *Israel and the Church*.

physical temple, destroyed and demolished in the first century AD, must be rebuilt in the city of Jerusalem and that this will be a paramount sign of God's faithfulness to Israel. In addition, many of them expect the Old Testament priestly system to be restored in some manner during the millennial kingdom. Even though certain historic premillennialists agree with some of these arguments, it seems that classical dispensational premillennialists too greatly emphasize the privileges of the Jews, without properly paying attention to the centrality of the church as "one new humanity" in God's redemptive economy.

The third major difficulty with classical dispensational premillennialism is its claim that the rapture will occur before the great tribulation. Even though classical dispensational premillennialists have been making every effort to prove their arguments for a pretribulational rapture, it seems that they have never been successful. Nowadays, a considerable number of dispensationalists are open to adopting a posttribulational or even midtribulational view of the rapture. They no longer want to be dogmatic about the pretribulational rapture, but want to maintain an open-ended attitude to evaluate other alternatives in a balanced manner. This is a great sign of maturation within classical dispensational circles.

Historical Development

It is not an overstatement to say that classical dispensational premillennialism is a revised version of historic premillennialism. Classical dispensational premillennialism agrees with historic premillennialism that the Lord Jesus Christ will establish the physical millennial kingdom on earth at the end of the great tribulation. As a matter of fact, this is a central commonality between classical dispensational and historic premillennialist views. However, it is important to appreciate the major differences between these two perspectives.

In this section, we will explore the history of classical dispensational premillennialism, from its origins with John Nelson

Darby to the modern day, focusing on major figures who made significant contributions to the propagation of this view.

John Nelson Darby (1800–1882)[10]

It is widely acknowledged that John Nelson Darby was the originator of classical dispensational premillennialism. Darby was an Irish Anglican priest. After resignation from his curacy, he became involved in the formation of the Plymouth Brethren, together with Anthony Norris Groves, Edward Cronin, J. G. Bellet, and Francis Hutchinson. Through the annual conferences at Powerscourt House, he began to preach publicly his own theological convictions regarding the notion of dispensations, the differences between the kingdom and the church, anticlericalism, antidenominationalism, the pretribulational rapture, and Calvinistic soteriology. Coining the term *dispensationalism*, he divided redemptive history into seven "dispensations": paradise, the Noahic dispensation, the Abrahamic dispensation, the dispensation of Israel, the dispensation of gentiles, the Spirit, and the millennium. He advocated a strictly literal approach to biblical and prophetic interpretation, the sharp distinction between Israel and the church, Christ's secret coming for the rapture of the church, and his second coming with his saints at the end of the great tribulation. With his profound knowledge of the original biblical languages, he also translated the Bible into many other modern languages.

He widely travelled all over England, Europe, North America, Australia, and New Zealand, preaching dispensational eschatology and propagating a view of biblical prophecies in this light. From 1862 to 1877, he partook in at least five missionary trips to North America, leading Bible conferences and revival meetings.

---

10. For biographical information about Darby, see Field, *John Nelson Darby*; and Weremchuk, *John Nelson Darby*.

James H. Brooks (1830–97)

James H. Brooks made an indelible contribution to the consolidation of dispensational premillennialism in America in the late nineteenth century. He ministered as pastor of Walnut Street Presbyterian Church in St. Louis, Missouri. More than anything else, he was one of the most influential leaders of Niagara Bible Conference, which played a crucial role in propagating pretribulational premillennialism throughout America. He worked together with Dwight L. Moody and mentored C. I. Scofield, the editor of the *Scofield Reference Bible*.[11] Brooks served as editor of *The Truth*, a magazine that also played a pivotal role in spreading classical dispensational premillennialism.

Dwight L. Moody (1837–1897)

D. L. Moody was an evangelist who led the third Great Awakening in America in the late nineteenth century.[12] He founded churches, schools, and publishing houses to spread the gospel. During his evangelistic trips to the United Kingdom, he encountered the Plymouth Brethren founded by John Nelson Darby and his colleagues. Moody accepted passionately Darby's dispensational and pretribulational premillennialism, and he made a significant contribution to its propagation despite his disagreement with Darby's Calvinistic soteriology.

C. I. Scofield (1843–1921)

Although the originator of dispensational premillennialism is John Nelson Darby, it is C. I. Scofield who made a decisive impact upon its popularization in North America. By attending Niagara Bible Conference, he was acquainted with Darby's dispensational eschatology. He was able to popularize classical dispensational

---

11. Scofield, ed., *Scofield Reference Bible*.
12. Cf. McLaughlin, *Revivals, Awakenings and Reform*.

premillennialism with the publishing of the *Scofield Reference Bible*, which he edited and through which he intended to propagate this view among ordinary believers—mostly fundamentalists.[13] After its initial publication in 1909, the *Scofield Reference Bible*—a study Bible annotated from the perspective of classical dispensational premillennialism—rapidly became the most popular and widespread means for the propagation of pretribulational premillennialism.

Scofield also assisted D. L. Moody in his evangelistic endeavors and was mentored by James H. Brooks. He founded the Philadelphia School of the Bible in Philadelphia, Pennsylvania, in order to train future church leaders, particularly from the perspective of classical dispensational premillennialism.

Arno C. Gaebelein (1861–1945)

Arno C. Gaebelein was a Methodist minister and a strong advocate of classical dispensational premillennialism in the early stages of its popularization. He assisted C. I. Scofield in the process of editing the *Scofield Reference Bible* and collaborated with him in the Niagara Bible Conferences. Gaebelein was a biblical scholar who published excellent works from the perspective of classical dispensational premillennialism. For example, he published *Current Events in the Light of the Bible* in 1914. In this book, he presented a robust case for interpreting the events of his days in light of biblical prophecies construed from a classical dispensational perspective. In addition, his magnum opus, *The Revelation: Analysis and Exposition of the Last Book of the Bible*, which was published in 1915, provided a comprehensive and integrative interpretation of the book of Revelation from the perspective of

---

13. On the history and impact of the Scofield Bible, see especially Mangum and Sweetnam, *The Scofield Bible*. For the relationship between dispensationalism and fundamentalism, see Marsden, *Fundamentalism and American Culture*.

classical dispensationalism. Furthermore, his work on the book of Daniel also exhibited this eschatological stance.[14]

Lewis Sperry Chafer (1871–1952)

Lewis Sperry Chafer was acquainted with C. I. Scofield from an early age and was even mentored by him. He helped Scofield in the process of founding the Philadelphia School of the Bible. In 1924, he founded Dallas Theological Seminary as a theological training center for future pastors, ministers, and missionaries and as a flagship school of classical dispensational premillennialism. From 1924 to his death in 1952, he served as both president of and professor of systematic theology at the seminary. In 1947, he published his magnum opus, *Systematic Theology*, which was soon to become the standard and authoritative textbook for classical dispensational theology.[15]

In this book, Chafer introduced a somewhat different set of dispensations than Darby did: innocence, conscience, human government, promise, law, grace, and kingdom rule,[16] presenting pretribulational premillennialism as the eschatological option most faithful to the teachings of Scripture. Darby did not present seven neatly structured dispensations. Rather, he regarded Noah, Abraham, Moses, and the Holy Spirit as the representatives of major dispensations. In addition, Chafer wrote *Dispensationalism*, a brief but profound introduction to dispensational theology. Through theological pamphlets such as *Must We Dismiss the Millennium?* (1921) and *The Kingdom in History and Prophecy* (1915), he expounded central themes of classical dispensational premillennialism.

---

14. Gaebelein, *Prophet Daniel*.
15. Chafer, *Systematic Theology*.
16. Ibid., 40–41.

Harry A. Ironside (1876–1951)

Harry A. Ironside was a Canadian American pastor and theologian who served Moody Church as senior pastor from 1929 to 1948. He was born into a family of Plymouth Brethren, and under the influence of Dwight L. Moody and C. I. Scofield, he championed classical dispensational premillennialism. His commentary on the book of Revelation, originally published in 1919,[17] and his book on the rapture,[18] published in 1941, confirmed the validity and veracity of dispensational premillennialism.

John F. Walvoord (1910–2002)

John F. Walvoord was a systematic theologian who served Dallas Theological Seminary as its president from 1952 to 1986. His specialty consisted in eschatology and he wrote major works on classical dispensational premillennialism. For example, he published *The Rapture Question* in 1957, in which he presented one of the most thorough and exhaustive cases for a pretribulational rapture. He also published *The Millennial Kingdom* in 1959, a comprehensive discussion of the theme of the millennium, in which he sought to demonstrate the veracity and validity of classical dispensational premillennialism, critically engaging with amillennialism and postmillennialism. In 1966 he published *The Revelation of Jesus Christ*, a commentary on the book of Revelation, in which he provided a profound case for classical dispensational premillennialism, interpreting verse by verse the most complex book of Scripture. Furthermore, in 1971 he published *Daniel: The Key to Prophetic Revelation*, in which he presented a dispensational premillennialist interpretation of the book of Daniel, expounding the theological significance of the prophecy of the seventy weeks in Daniel 9 for eschatology.[19] In addition, he published *The Blessed Hope and the Tribulation: A Historical*

---

17. Ironside, *Revelation*.
18. Ironside, *Not Wrath but Rapture*.
19. Walvoord, *Daniel*, 201–37.

and Biblical Study of Posttribulationalism in 1976, in which he attempted to prove that pretribulational premillennialism is the best interpretation of the biblical evidence for the rapture's timing, criticizing different versions of posttribulationalism on the basis of historical and biblical research.

J. Dwight Pentecost (1915–2014)

J. Dwight Pentecost served Dallas Theological Seminary as Distinguished Professor of Bible Exposition during his tenure there from 1955 to 2014. Whereas John F. Walvoord was the representative systematic theologian in the camp of classical dispensational premillennialism, Pentecost was the representative biblical expositor in the camp. He published his magnum opus, *Things to Come: A Study in Biblical Eschatology* in 1958, in which he thoroughly discussed major themes of dispensational premillennialism, including the method of prophetic interpretation, the theories of the rapture, the great tribulation, and the millennial kingdom. This book became a bestseller and sold hundreds of thousands of copies.

In addition, Pentecost published *Thy Kingdom Come: Tracing God's Kingdom Program and Covenant Promises throughout History* in 1995, in which he presented one of the most comprehensive and thorough discussions of God's plan and providence in relation to the kingdom from a classical dispensational premillennial perspective.

Charles Caldwell Ryrie (1925–2016)

Charles Caldwell Ryrie served Dallas Theological Seminary as Professor of Systematic Theology and Cairn University as president and a professor. He is regarded as one of the best-known champions of classical dispensational premillennialism. He edited and published *The Ryrie Study Bible* in 1978, which sold more than two million copies.

Ryrie wrote other significant works on classical dispensational premillennialism as well. In 1966, he published *Dispensationalism Today*, where he presented basic beliefs of classical dispensational premillennialism. Expanding this book, he wrote *Dispensationalism* in 1995, in which he discussed hermeneutical features and major beliefs of classical dispensational premillennialism, comparing it with progressive dispensationalism and covenant theology. Furthermore, he wrote *The Basis of the Premillennial Faith* in 1981. This book delineated the hermeneutical principles of classical dispensational premillennialism and expounded its fundamental beliefs, such as the pretribulational rapture and the millennial kingdom on earth. In addition, he published *Come Quickly Lord Jesus: What You Need to Know about the Rapture* in 1996, in which he advocated a pretribulational rapture, criticizing other options.

Hal Lindsay (1929–)

Hal Lindsay is a Christian writer with dispensational persuasions, educated at Dallas Theological Seminary. He made a very significant contribution to the propagation of classical dispensational premillennialism among ordinary Christians in North America and beyond. In particular, in 1970, he published *The Late Great Planet Earth*,[20] which was soon to become a best seller. In this book, he presented an interpretation of contemporary events in view of biblical prophecies about the last days from a classical dispensational premillennial perspective. For example, he argued that the establishment of the national state of Israel in 1948 was a fulfillment of biblical prophecies that foresaw ethnic Jews returning to their old land when the last period of human history began. Furthermore, he also contended that the foundation of the European Economic Community would result in the formation of the ten nations of Revelation 17:10–13. The confederation of these ten nations, he argued, will be the revived Roman Empire and will give power to the Antichrist who will reign the whole

---

20. Lindsey wrote this book with C. C. Carlson.

world as a violent dictator, severely persecuting the Jews left behind after the rapture of the church.

Hal Lindsey wrote another book, *The 1980s: Countdown to Armageddon*, in which he presented a dispensational premillennialist interpretation of current events in the world, particularly in the Middle East. In this book, he made a bold prediction that the Antichrist was already on earth and would even rise in the 1980s, along with some decisive events related to biblical prophecies about the last days of human history. Because his prediction has proven false, he has become an object of severe criticism from those who have different eschatological persuasions. In addition, in 1983 he published *The Rapture: Truth or Consequences*, where he advocated the classical dispensational premillennialist view of the pretribulational rapture.

Tim LaHaye and Jerry B. Jenkins: The *Left Behind* Series

Tim LaHaye (1926–2016) and Jerry B. Jenkins (1949–) coauthored a series of fictional, apocalyptic novels, the *Left Behind* series (1995–2007),[21] on the basis of classical dispensational premillennialism. These novels provide a fictional drama about those who will be left behind after the rapture of the church. The series has become the most influential literary product in the propagation of classical dispensational premillennialism among not only common Christians but also unbelievers. It has been translated into a variety of different languages and continues to gain worldwide attention and support today.[22]

---

21. LaHaye and Jenkins, *Left Behind Series*.

22. These books were translated and marketed in Korea as well; interestingly, they did not fare so well commercially in Korea as they did in the United States.

John F. MacArthur (1939–)

John F. MacArthur is a pastor, theologian, and educator. Currently, he is serving as pastor of Grace Community Church and president of the Master's University and Theological Seminary in California. He has been widely known as one of the most influential expository preachers for the last fifty years. His theology is Calvinistic and Reformed, but his eschatology is classical dispensational premillennialist. He has written several significant books related to classical dispensational premillennialism. For example, in 1999 he published *The Second Coming: Signs of Christ's Return and the End of Age*, in which he provided an exposition of Matthew 24 from a classical dispensationalist perspective. He also demonstrated his dispensational premillennialism by arguing that the rapture of the church will occur before the great tribulation.

In addition, in 2007 he published *Because the Time Is Near: John MacArthur Explains the Book of Revelation*, a detailed exposition of Revelation from a classical dispensational premillennial perspective. Furthermore, together with theologian Richard Mayhue, he edited and published *Christ's Prophetic Plans: A Futuristic Premillennial Primer* in 2012, in which contributors provided a robust case for classical dispensational premillennialism.

Watchman Nee (1903–72)

Watchman Nee is regarded as one of the most influential Christian leaders in twentieth-century China. He was a dynamic minister, inspirational writer, and profound expositor of the Bible. His biblical and theological writings have significantly influenced numerous Christians, not only in China, but also in Asia and beyond.[23]

Through his mentor Margaret E. Barber (1866–1930),[24] a British missionary to China, Nee was introduced to the Plymouth Brethren and the dispensational theology of John Nelson Darby in his twenties. He remained a classical dispensational

---

23. See Laurent, *Watchman Nee*.
24. For her biography, see Reetzke, *M. E. Barber*.

premillennialist throughout his life.[25] Of course, his eschatological beliefs were not exactly the same as Darby's, but it would be safe to say that Nee was a dispensational pretribulational premillennialist. Moreover, Nee's powerful ministry was a major catalyst in the spread of dispensational premillennialism among Chinese evangelicals.

David (Paul) Yonggi Cho (1936–)

David Yonggi Cho is a world-renowned Pentecostal leader who has been ministering, since the 1970s, to Yoido Full Gospel Church in South Korea, the largest single congregation in the world with a membership of over 800,000. His ministry has been profoundly influential, not only in South Korea, but also around the globe. Through numerous books and pamphlets, he has been advocating the miraculous work of the Holy Spirit and the theology of threefold blessings, including wellbeing of the soul, prosperity and health, and the spirituality of the fourth dimension. He has been the object of hot debate among Christian theologians, and the orthodoxy of his theology and spirituality have been seriously questioned. However, it seems undeniable that he endorses the doctrine of the Trinity, Christ's deity and humanity, his vicarious atonement, his resurrection, and his second coming. This makes him an orthodox theologian. Of course, his predilections and propensities toward the prosperity gospel should be critically evaluated.

In terms of eschatology, David Yonggi Cho has been a strong advocate of classical dispensational premillennialism. In 1990, he presented a classical dispensational interpretation of Daniel 9 and the theme of seventy weeks with the publication of his commentary on the book of Daniel.[26] In 1992, he also published a commentary on the book of Revelation in which he presented a strong case for classical dispensational premillennialism.[27] Moreover, in 1998

25. Wu, *Understanding Watchman Nee*, 51–82.
26. Cho, *Daniel*.
27. Cho, *Revelation*.

he wrote *The Apocalyptic Prophecy: Reconciling Today's Global Events with End-Time Prophecy*, in which he attempted to interpret contemporary world events in line with biblical prophecies from a classical dispensational premillennial perspective.

Conclusion

Classical dispensational premillennialism shares the same roots as historic premillennialism, claiming that the parousia will occur prior to the establishment of the millennial kingdom on earth. However, it has its own unique features that cannot be easily harmonized or reconciled with other premillennial models such as historic premillennialism. It is important to appreciate, therefore, that these distinctive characteristics have been sources of both attraction and aversion. Many people have been drawn to classical dispensational premillennialism because of its visions for the blessed future of the Jews and its good news with respect to the church's escape from the great tribulation. Moreover, its propensity to connect current global events with biblical prophecies has been an important and fascinating factor that has contributed to its global propagation. However, that very tendency to link the Bible with current events has led others to express animosity and antipathy toward it.

In this vein, the relevant question is still whether classical dispensational premillennialism is faithful to the teachings of Scripture. Of course, classical dispensational premillennialists would argue that their positons and beliefs are the products of genuine and authentic efforts at remaining faithful to the Word of God. However, they should maintain an open and generous attitude toward criticisms from other eschatological camps because those criticisms seem to be appropriate and pertinent in light of the biblical evidence. Therefore, it is the responsibility for all of us to test and examine the Scriptures to see if what classical dispensational premillennialism says is true. In so doing, we need to learn how to accept what is truthful in it and to set aside what is not.

3

Progressive Dispensationalism

—David L. Mathewson

Introduction

THE PURPOSE OF THIS chapter is to examine the view of the millennium in Revelation 20 as articulated by progressive dispensationalism. The movement known as dispensationalism, by definition, is premillennial. This also includes the development and revision within dispensationalism known as "progressive dispensationalism." There are both similarities and stark differences between the role the millennium plays in progressive dispensationalism and the view of the millennium in more classic forms of dispensationalism. The purpose of this section is not primarily to compare the two, but rather to tease out the perspective of progressive dispensationalism on the millennium, especially its treatment of Revelation 20:4–6.

There are three primary figures who have been at the forefront of the origin and development of this movement known as progressive dispensationalism by virtue of their groundbreaking publications. All of them teach or have taught at schools traditionally associated with classic dispensationalism: Darrell Bock (Dallas Seminary), Craig Blaising (Southwestern Baptist Theological Seminary, formerly of Dallas Seminary), and Robert Saucy

(Talbot Seminary).[1] But others have "jumped on board" and have embraced some form of progressive dispensationalism.[2] Unlike more classical expressions, progressive dispensationalists generally agree that the OT prophecies of a coming *messianic kingdom are being fulfilled already at the first coming of Christ*. That is, at his first coming Christ not only offered, but brought to fulfillment the OT promises of a coming kingdom. Yet the promised kingdom was only initially and partially realized, and still has a consummate, future fulfillment. "The kingdom promised in the Old Testament, with its central features in the Davidic covenant, thus finds its fulfillment according to the New Testament teaching both in the present church age and in the future."[3] In other words, progressive dispensationalism is consistent with the "already" but "not yet" tension of realized and futuristic eschatology that was popularized by G. E. Ladd and has come to characterize the mainstream of NT scholarship. With the first coming of Christ, his death, resurrection, and ascension, the promised messianic, Davidic kingdom from the OT has arrived. Yet it has not yet come in its final, consummate form. The final form of the kingdom still awaits its fulfillment with the second coming of Christ in the future. Therefore, the OT promises of a coming messianic kingdom are fulfilled progressively, first in Jesus and his death and resurrection, then in the church as the people of the Messiah, then in a further stage in the millennial kingdom, and finally in its consummate stage in the new heaven and new earth (Revelation 21–22). All of these are instances of progressive stages of fulfillment of the single messianic kingdom prophesied in the OT. It is important to add that for progressive dispensationalism the initial fulfillment of the kingdom is a genuine *fulfillment*, not just an *application* of some of the spiritual aspects of the kingdom.

1. Bock and Blaising, *Progressive Dispensationalism*; Saucy, *Progressive Dispensationalism*.

2. See the collection of essays in Blaising and Bock, eds., *Dispensationalism, Israel, and the Church*.

3. Saucy, *Progressive Dispensationalism*, 110.

Hermeneutical Principles

Progressive dispensationalism shows significant hermeneutical development and advances over its classical cousin. First, progressive dispensationalists emphasize even more than classical dispensationalism a *unified redemptive plan* of God that embraces both Jews and gentiles and that embraces both physical/political and spiritual realities; in other words, its approach is more *holistic*. "In progressive dispensationalism, the political-social and spiritual purposes of God complement one another."[4] Regarding the kingdom of God, there are not two separate kingdoms, a spiritual kingdom and a physical kingdom with attendant spiritual and physical blessings respectively, but one kingdom with both physical/material and spiritual dimensions. Jesus's "concept of the kingdom was that of the Old Testament prophecies which included spiritual, physical, and political dimensions, especially the restoration of the nation of Israel."[5] Assuming the progressive nature of fulfillment, this means that some of the aspects, physical and spiritual, could be fulfilled in an initial installment, while other features, both spiritual and physical, await a future, consummate fulfillment.

Second, and related to the previous observation, progressive dispensationalists see the church as fulfilling OT prophecy and therefore participating in the same promises of salvation as Jews. There is not the sharp distinction between Israel and the church that characterized classic dispensationalism. However, this does not rule out a specific role for Israel in the future (i.e., in the millennium) for progressive dispensationalists, but it refuses to find in Scripture one redemptive plan and set of promises for Israel and another separate set for the church. So the Davidic kingdom promised in the OT already finds fulfillment in the church age, even though it still awaits its final consummate fulfillment. Therefore, the quotation of or allusion to OT texts such as Psalms 2 and 110 in the NT (see Acts 2:34–35; Eph 1: 20–23; Heb 1:5, 13) demonstrate that at his ascension Christ actually

---

4. Bock and Blaising, *Progressive Dispensationalism*, 48.
5. Saucy, *Progressive Dispensationalism*, 89.

entered into his Davidic rule in fulfillment of the OT promises.[6] Jesus is the heir to the Davidic covenant and its promises. For progressives, "*the Davidic nature of Christ's present activity guarantees the fulfillment of all of the Davidic promise in the future, including the national and political dimensions of that promise.*"[7] Third, progressive dispensationalism has made significant hermeneutical advances in interpretation of biblical texts. The main development has been the tendency to move away from the term "literal" that characterized the classic dispensational approach to interpreting biblical prophetic texts. There is now a tempering of this with a more consistent interpretive approach that is historical and literary. Especially significant for our purposes is the role that literary genre plays in the hermeneutics of progressive dispensationalism. That is, literary genre determines and influences heuristically how one approaches a given biblical text. Bock and Blaising recognize the importance that literary genre plays by comparing it to a sporting event: "each game is played by its own rules and has its own expectations about how to play the game. The variety of literature is the same way."[8] With regard to two important literary genres for our purposes, prophecies "rely heavily on symbolic imagery to make their points."[9] In their treatment of apocalyptic literature, Bock and Blaising describe it as "heavily symbolic literature." Therefore, both types of literature are not to be interpreted literally, but according to their literary genre. This does not mean that prophetic or apocalyptic texts like Revelation do not refer to actual, literal events—they can and do. But it does mean that apocalyptic literature paints reality rather than describing it. So literary genre plays a crucial role in how the interpreter comes to the biblical text. These are significant advances, and pave the way for important developments in the progressive dispensational view of the millennium.

6. Bock, "Covenant in Progressive Dispensationalism," 169–203.
7. Bock and Blaising, *Progressive Dispensationalism*, 180. Italics theirs.
8. Bock and Blaising, *Progressive Dispensationalism*, 85.
9. Bock and Blaising, *Progressive Dispensationalism*, 89.

OT Prophecies

Progressive dispensationalists obviously give particular attention to OT prophecies anticipating a messianic kingdom, with Jerusalem and its cult at the center, where the Messiah will defeat his enemies and rule over his people in righteousness and justice (Isa 9:7). God's rule over Israel and all nations will take place from Zion through his Messiah (Isa 2:2–4; Mic 4:7; cf. Psalm 2). Israel will be restored to its land in a new covenant relationship with God (Ezek 37:24–28) and will play an important role of being a light to all the nations of the earth (Isaiah 60). Thus, the promises of a future kingdom contain both physical/political and spiritual aspects. In summary, the OT anticipates a time when "God will establish a worldwide kingdom on earth centered in Jerusalem in which He and His Messiah, a descendant of David, will rule Israel and all nations."[10] As seen above, the prophecies find valid fulfillment, particularly in their spiritual dimensions and blessings, in Jesus and his people, the church, consisting of redeemed Jews and gentiles. Jesus is the heir to the Davidic covenant and promises, and all covenants find their fulfillment in him. The blessings of the Abrahamic, Davidic, and new covenant "are given in a partial and inaugurated form."[11] But they are indeed given and fulfilled directly in the present, not just *applied* to the church. Jesus comes as king and offers the initial phase of the OT theocratic, Davidic kingdom. His ascension into heaven where he sits on his throne is the throne promised to David in the OT (Ps 110:1). According to Saucy,

> This interpretation of the exaltation of Jesus to the right hand of God in fulfillment of the Davidic messianic promise therefore allows for the inaugural fulfillment of those promises in distinction from the total postponement of the Davidic promise in traditional dispensationalism.... To interpret Psalm 110, in regard to the kingship of Christ, as expressing a dimension of

---

10. Bock and Blaising, *Progressive Dispensationalism*, 228.
11. Bock and Blaising, *Progressive Dispensationalism*, 53.

fulfillment in the present age and another dimension in the future harmonizes well with the overall picture that the eschatological prophecies of the Old Testament are fulfilled in several stages without losing their basic historical meaning.[12]

Bock and Blaising conclude that "The Messiah has been raised up, seated (enthroned) at the right hand of God, all things, specifically all rule and authority, have been subjected to Him, and He is building the house of God."[13] Therefore, the church is a "present reality of the coming eschatological kingdom."[14] In Saucy's words:

> The believer is related to this kingdom [Davidic messianic kingdom promised in the OT] through faith in the King and is therefore an heir and already a citizen of the coming kingdom. The King has already bestowed some of the blessings of the kingdom on its citizens, so it is possible to speak of the presence of the kingdom now.[15]

Saucy appears to be slightly different from Bock and Blaising, in that he thinks that the full spiritual and physical/political kingdom was indeed offered in Jesus's early ministry, but was rejected by the hearers (whereas Bock and Blaising think that the kingdom was only offered in initial, inaugurated form). After it was rejected, Jesus then taught, especially in the kingdom parables (e.g., Matthew 13), that the kingdom promised in the OT would still be present (and fulfilled), but in a limited form rather than in its full eschatological form, which would now be delayed for a future time.[16] In this way, he is somewhat similar to classical dispensationalism, which thought that Jesus offered the kingdom of God to Israel, they rejected it, and God postponed or delayed it until the future. The difference is that Saucy still finds a valid *fulfillment* of the promises of the kingdom, even in a limited way, actually in

---

12. Saucy, *Progressive Dispensationalism*, 76.
13. Bock and Blaising, *Progressive Dispensationalism*, 259.
14. Bock and Blaising, *Progressive Dispensationalism*, 258.
15. Saucy, *Progressive Dispensationalism*, 110.
16. Saucy, *Progressive Dispensationalism*, 86–87.

the present. According to progressive dispensationalists, then, "the church can exist as a distinct institution in the plan of God and yet can share in promises originally given to Israel, because God brings them into the promise through his plan involving Christ the seed of Abraham, who also was the promised vehicle through whom the world would be blessed (Galatians 3–4)."[17]

However, the physical and political elements of the kingdom are still taken seriously, and can only be fulfilled in a future earthly kingdom. "God can say more in his development of promises from the OT to the NT, but not less."[18] "The present dispensation is not the full and complete revelation of the eschatological kingdom. It is a progressive stage in the revelation of that kingdom."[19] There is still a future fulfillment that will encompass the OT promises of a kingdom in all their spiritual and physical/political dimensions. Therefore, it is illegitimate simply to spiritualize the OT promises of a coming kingdom where Israel plays a distinct role. Nor is it appropriate to land the promises in the eternal state (as is typical in amillennialism). The OT promises of a coming kingdom seem to anticipate a this-worldly kingdom; that is, it must find fulfillment in this present earth, not in the new creation or eternal state (Revelation 21–22). Emphasis on one people of God and one redemptive plan of God does not entail abandoning a role for restored, national Israel in the outworking of the establishment of God's kingdom (see Romans 11). "The notion of a political, earthly kingdom has not dropped out or been resignified."[20] Thus, progressive dispensationalists still insist on 1) a future for ethnic, restored Israel; 2) a distinction between Israel and the church, not as two separate peoples, but "as functioning institutions throughout the plan of God."[21] This is part of the rationale for the need of a future, millennial kingdom on this earth, a stage of the kingdom that progressives find clearly taught in Revelation 20:4–6.

17. Bock and Blaising, *Progressive Dispensationalism*, 85.
18. Bock, "Why I Am a Dispensationalist with a Small 'd,'" 390.
19. Bock and Blaising, *Progressive Dispensationalism*, 260.
20. Bock and Blaising, *Progressive Dispensationalism*, 237.
21. Bock and Blaising, *Progressive Dispensationalism*, 260.

Interpretation of Revelation 20

Revelation 20:4–6

This brings us to the only biblical text that mentions the millennium explicitly. Though the understanding of the significance of the millennium by progressive dispensationalists depends on far more than just an exegesis of Revelation 20:4–6 (resting also on broader issues of interpretation of OT texts and a conception of the outworking of the overall redemptive plan of God in history), Revelation 20:4–6 still plays a key role in the discussion, since it is the only text in the OT and NT that unambiguously teaches a thousand-year reign. Like classical dispensationalists, progressive dispensationalists see Revelation 20:4–6 as anticipating a future, earthly kingdom. Both amillennial and premillennial (excluding classic dispensationalists) approaches to the kingdom agree that there are two primary phases to the fulfillment of the OT promises of a kingdom: an initial, *present* phase in Christ and the church, and a *future* eschatological phase in the new creation (Revelation 21–22). Premillennialists go one step further and find that *the future eschatological phase of the kingdom also comes in two stages*: a millennial kingdom followed temporally by the final perfected form of the kingdom in the new creation.[22] As Saucy summarizes,

> According to amillennialist teaching, the future fulfillment of the kingdom contains essentially one phase. Christ will return to bring about the full salvation of his people and the judgment of the lost, after which the final eternal kingdom will be ushered in. For premillennialists, however, the future of the kingdom involves two phases. Christ will come and establish his kingdom on earth, which will be a glorious reign over an as-yet imperfect world. Only after this time will he deliver the kingdom over to the Father to usher in the perfect state.[23]

---

22. Saucy, *Progressive Dispensationalism*, 272.
23. Saucy, *Progressive Dispensationalism*, 272.

Many of the progressive dispensationalists' arguments for a future millennium would resemble other premillennial positions, such as classical dispensationalism and historic premillennialism, since they all share in common a view of the millennium as a distinct period of time in the future (as opposed to amillennialism) that separates the second coming of Christ and the eternal state (new creation).[24] Thus, for example, 1) the sequential nature of Revelation 19:11—21:8, which records events that take place during or after the second coming (19:11–21), 2) the two (physical) resurrections (20:4, 5, 11–14) separated by an interval of a thousand years, 3) the complete binding of Satan (20:1–3) so that he can no longer deceive the nations, all can argue for a future millennial kingdom.[25]

Furthermore, "a future restoration [of Israel] in itself seems to imply a millennial phase of the kingdom."[26] According to Bock and Blaising, the reference to the two resurrections in Revelation 20 is specific and has an "Israelite feel" to it.[27] A future millennial reign is also consistent with predictions of a coming eschatological kingdom elsewhere in the NT, as well as the promise that Jesus's followers would rule over the twelve tribes of Israel in the future (Matt 19:28; see 1 Cor 6:2). The millennium functions as a transitional stage between the second coming of Christ in Revelation 19:11–21 and the establishment of the new creation in 21:1—22:5, as well as between the present form of the kingdom in Christ and his church and the eternal kingdom (21:1—22:5).[28] Progressive dispensationalists admit that a future millennial kingdom is only explicitly taught in Revelation 20.[29] However, there is one other text

---

24. Post-millennialism, like premillennialism, also sees a future kingdom on this earth. But unlike premillennial approaches, this view sees Christ's return as occurring *after* (post) the millennium that will be set up on earth through the church and the work of the Holy Spirit.

25. For further details see Blaising, "Premillennialism," 212–27.

26. Saucy, *Progressive Dispensationalism*, 273.

27. Bock and Blaising, *Progressive Dispensationalism*, 93.

28. Saucy, *Progressive Dispensationalsim*, 212.

29. Bock and Blaising, *Progressive Dispensationalism*, 273: "Revelation 20 is the only Scripture that *explicitly* predicts (or envisions) an *intermediate*,

that may also point in that direction. In 1 Corinthians 15:23-25 Paul envisions progressive stages of the resurrection and establishment of the kingdom. The text envisions the coming of the "end" after the future resurrection of the people of God. The key phrase is "he must reign until he has put all his enemies under his feet" (v. 25), which statement comes after the reference to "the end" in v. 24. This seems to indicate a period of time ("the end") before the final, eternal kingdom, and this is a period of time where Christ must reign until he has vanquished all his enemies. While this text does not require a millennial period of time that precedes the end, it is certainly suggestive and compatible with it.[30]

But the key text is still Revelation 20:1-6. Revelation 19:11-21 is the climax of John's Apocalypse, where the coming of Christ to earth to judge his enemies is portrayed. In any typical premillennial reading of this section, the rest of chapters 20-22 depicts a further sequence of events that will transpire at the time of or following Christ's coming. The fact that Satan's deceptive activity from which he is bound takes place on earth suggests that the reign of the saints in 20:4-6 will be on earth as well.[31]

Like the OT, the NT looks forward to an eschatological kingdom, where God will rule from Jerusalem over all the nations on a new earth in Revelation 21:1—22:5. This text from Revelation is shot through with OT allusions to prophetic texts which anticipate a restored Israel and restored Jerusalem with God dwelling in the midst of his people in a new creation (e.g., Ezekiel 37, 40-48; Isaiah 60, 65, Zechariah 14), where the throne of God and the Lamb are at its center.[32] The rule is both spiritual and political and will include all nations as well as Israel. But the "millennial kingdom constitutes another stage in the revelation of the eschatological kingdom."[33]

---

millennial kingdom. No other passage speaks implicitly or explicitly about a *millennial* kingdom, that is a kingdom lasting 1,000 years." Italics theirs.

30. Blaising, "Premillennialsim," 203-4; Saucy, *Progressive Dispensationalism*, 280-83.

31. Saucy, *Progressive Dispensationalism*, 277.

32. Mathewson, *New Heaven and a New Earth*.

33. Bock and Blaising, *Progressive Dispensationalism*, 270.

Though a thousand-year kingdom is explicitly predicted in the NT only in Revelation 20, it is nonetheless seen as consistent with earlier OT and NT anticipations of the coming eschatological kingdom.[34] Thus, progressive dispensationalists point to those OT texts, such as Psalm 2, where the Messiah is to rule over the earth, and Isaiah 65:17–20, which still envisions imperfection and death in the future establishment of the kingdom. The OT gives evidence of a kingdom where the Messiah rules from Jerusalem over an imperfect world (e.g., Ezek 44:25, 27).[35] This could only happen in a period prior to the perfected eternal state (new creation). This is consistent with what progressive dispensationalists find in Revelation 20, where the Messiah and his saints rule, but where sin and death have not yet been completely eliminated (see Rev 20:8–11). The millennium is a further stage of the establishment of God's kingdom that is now revealed in the progressive revelation of God's plan for redemption, but which is consistent with earlier revelation of a future kingdom on earth. "Because dispensationalists consider these Old Testament prophecies—including those related to the nation of Israel—still valid, a millennium is vital and integral to their view of the future of the kingdom promises, perhaps more so than other premillennialists."[36] Following the fulfillment of the kingdom in the life of Christ and in the establishment of the church, the millennium is understood as "a 1,000-year intermediate kingdom during which Christ rules on earth prior to and as a step toward the final fulfillment of the everlasting promises." (271). It is during this millennial reign that the earthly kingdom will be fully manifested in all its spiritual and political dimensions. Bock and Blaising summarize the state of affairs present during the millennium:

> The resurrected Christ and resurrected saints (cf. Dan. 7:14, 27; 12:2) will administer human life on the earth in its national and political dimensions. As Messiah of Israel, Jesus will fulfill for that nation the promises

---

34. Blaising, "Premillennialism," 200.
35. Saucy, *Progressive Dispensationalism*, 230, 241, 272–73.
36. Saucy, *Progressive Dispensationalism*, 273.

covenanted to her, and He will rule over all nations so that through Him all nations might be blessed. He will rule with "a rod of iron," imprisoning spiritual wickedness and subjugating all human authority to Himself. The spiritual blessings which were displayed in the previous dispensation in the life of the eschatological community, the church, will be extended in this stage of the kingdom through national and political dimensions of human life as well. The earthly blessings which were glimpsed in individual messianic works during the first advent will be extended around the world. At the end of this stage of the kingdom, evil itself will be destroyed in a display of Christ's judgment against satanic and human rebellion, and death along with sin will be elimination.[37]

Following the millennial kingdom, "the eschatological kingdom of God in all its fullness will be manifest eternal and immortal on a renewed earth."[38] Therefore, progressive dispensationalism exhibits a unified view of the millennium from Revelation 20 situated within the progressive, redemptive outworking of the establishment of God's kingdom on earth. The millennium in Revelation 20 is not understood as a distinct entity unrelated to much of Christ's earthly ministry, the church, and the eternal state (Revelation 21–22), but finds its unifying framework within the overall outworking of God's redemptive plan that includes Jew and gentile, as well as material, political, physical, and spiritual blessings. The millennial kingdom from Revelation 20 is to be identified with the messianic kingdom of OT prophecy. But it is only one stage in its fulfillment. The kingdom of God is implemented progressively in stages, with the millennium functioning as only one stage (albeit a very important one) in the progressive outworking of God's kingdom in all its physical and spiritual aspects, yet a stage where Israel plays a particular *role* in mediating blessings to all the nations. There is both continuity and discontinuity between the new creation and this present creation, so that the new creation is the ultimate fulfillment of the *earthly* promises of the

37. Bock and Blaising, *Progressive Dispensationalism*, 282–83.
38. Bock and Blaising, *Progressive Dispensationalism*, 283.

OT. Therefore, in progressive dispensationalism, the millennium does not play *the* central role that it does in classical dispensational approaches, but it does play a more important role in relationship to the OT promises of the Messiah reigning from restored Israel than historical premillennial approaches.[39]

The Rationale for a Millennium

As seen above, in progressive dispensational premillennialism, the millennial stage of the kingdom is only one stage, which gives way to the final fulfillment in the eternal state. This raises the potential question of why the need for a separate stage of fulfillment in a millennial reign. Saucy asks, "Is there any reason for such a temporary interval between the present, initial phase of the kingdom and its final consummation?"[40] Why not just skip right to the final, eschatological phase of the kingdom in the new heavens and new earth (i.e., amillennialism)? (Actually this question applies to all forms of premillennialism that wish to see an extended period of time where God's OT promises of a messianic kingdom are fulfilled.) Therefore, it is important to consider the rationale for a millennial kingdom in the progressive dispensational scheme. At its heart, the progressive dispensational view of the millennium depends on more than just a certain exegesis of Revelation 20:4–6. It also depends on an understanding of the overall redemptive plan of God in the OT and NT, as well as the theological rationale for a millennial kingdom in relationship to that framework. This is where their distinctive approach to the millennium can be discerned. The following rationale have already been highlighted in the previous discussion, and will only be summarized here. First, Saucy notes that the prominence and centrality of Christ must be seen *in history*, not in a later eternal state. Christ's prominence and sovereignty must be vindicated on this earth. At present that

---

39. This is one of the criticisms of progressive dispensationalism "internally" by a proponent of classic dispensationalism; Ryrie, *Dispensationalism*, 177–78.

40. Saucy, *Progressive Dispensationalism*, 289.

prominence remains hidden and must be openly acknowledged and become visible *in history*. "The millennial kingdom reign of Christ emphasizes the central place in history of the person and work of Christ."[41] The millennium answers the need for "the historical manifestation of Christ's triumph."[42] Second, "a future reign of the Messiah on earth is necessary for the completion of all that God has promised through the Messiah."[43] The transformation of all things, the manifestation of peace and God's righteousness *in this world* (not just in the eternal state or world to come) would seem to require a future millennial reign on this earth.

Third, related to this, this is where the physical, earthly OT promises given to Israel will be fulfilled. The restoration of Israel as a nation according to OT prophetic texts would seem to require a period of time on this earth in the future where Israel would play a prominent role among the nations. A future for national Israel is what primarily distinguishes a progressive dispensational approach to the millennium from a historical premillennial approach:

> Progressives go one step further than historical premillennialists in arguing that the millennial kingdom anticipates an administrative structure where national Israel again assumes a central place as the home of the reigning Messiah, in the midst of the nations who also respond to the Christ. Progressives do not argue this point in such a way as to deny the fundamental equality of Jew and Gentile in the benefits of salvation. So progressives speak openly, as other dispensationalists do, of a future for *national* Israel among the nations in the Millennium. It is this detail that makes a premillennial view dispensational.[44]

Thus, progressive dispensationalists take the OT promises seriously, and find their fulfillment in an earthly millennium prior to

---

41. Saucy, *Progressive Dispensationalism*, 289.
42. Saucy, *Progressive Dispensationalism*, 291.
43. Saucy, *Progressive Dispensationalism*, 291–92.
44. Bock, "Summary Essay," 292.

the establishment of the new creation (Revelation 21–22), however much the latter is still the consummate stage of the kingdom. This earthly millennium predicted in Revelation 20 is where the OT promises of an earthly kingdom promised to restored, national Israel are going to be fulfilled. "Because dispensationalists consider these Old Testament prophecies—including those related to the nation of Israel—still valid, a millennium is vital and integral to their view of the future of the kingdom promises, perhaps more so than other premillennialists."[45]

Critical Engagement

While progressive dispensational approaches to the millennium have certainly made advances on and answered some of the weaknesses of classical dispensational views, their treatment of the millennium still raises a number of questions. First, Revelation 20 itself is quite *vague* about what happens in millennium. There is no clear mention of who is there, of what takes place there, and certainly no clear mention of a restored Israel and the fulfillment of Israel's promises. This does not mean that it is invalid to draw conclusions regarding the nature of the millennium. But from a literary standpoint, is it reading *into* Revelation 20 to find OT promises of the land and the restoration of Israel fulfilled? What is interesting is that if Revelation is followed closely—and Revelation 20 must at least form our starting point for our understanding of the millennium—all the occurrences of OT texts about the restoration of Israel and the promised blessings of the kingdom are found in Revelation 21:1—22:5, *not* in Revelation 20:4–6. Progressive dispensationalism simply *assumes* that the millennium in Revelation 20 is to be identified with the messianic kingdom prophesied in the OT. Second, though it is important for progressive dispensationalists to find fulfillment of the OT's earthly promises to Israel in the millennium of Revelation 20:4–6, the text itself is not clear *where* the millennium even takes place. It could be on earth, but

---

45. Saucy, *Progressive Dispensationalism*, 273.

it could also be in heaven. Revelation 20:4-6 is ambiguous in this regard. So it may be making the text bear too much by insisting on an *earthly* fulfillment of Israel's promises taking place during the millennium. Again, one must assume that the millennium is the fulfillment of the OT promises of a messianic kingdom, and read the millennium in light of the broader progressive establishment of God's kingdom on earth.

Furthermore, progressive dispensationalism understands the millennium with the Jew/gentile distinction still in place, though not to the same degree that classical dispensationalism does (for there are not two separate peoples, but one people with Israel playing a distinct role as a light to the nations). This is inevitable given the way they put all the pieces of the puzzle together and understand the relationship of OT prophecy to its fulfillment in the NT. Yet everyone must "fit" the millennium into the broader redemptive-historical fulfillment of God's promises of a coming kingdom. Yet others might understand the relationship between the OT and NT differently, and put the pieces of the puzzle together differently.

Finally, why cannot final redemption in all its spiritual and physical/political dimensions take place on the new *earth* (Revelation 21-22)? Along with classic dispensational approaches, progressive dispensationalists seem to think that the OT promises of restoration and vindication must at some level take place in this world, not in the eternal state. However, this assumes a far more significant amount of discontinuity between the present earth and the new creation in Revelation 21:1—22:5 than may be warranted, and overlooks the significant continuity between the two. Only if we completely separate the two creations, or at least downplay the relationship between the two, and end history at the close of the millennium is this a problem. Rather, the new creation of Revelation 21-22 is *this creation* renewed, restored, and vindicated. It is the entire goal towards which God's redemptive plan, which embraces all creation, is moving,[46] in the same way that our resurrection bodies are the final restoration and ultimate vindication of the people of

46. See Bauckham, *Theology of Revelation*, 132-43.

God. It is not some separate entity after God's plan for this present world has been accomplished. It is not some eternal state that lies out there beyond history. All the OT texts of restoration are found in Revelation 21:1—22:5 rather than in Revelation 20:4–6. The new creation (which is *this* world transformed, renewed) is where Christ is seen to be Lord of all; this is where creation is vindicated; this is where the purposes of God *for history* find their fulfillment; this is where people of God, Jews and gentiles, find ultimate fulfillment of OT promises of restoration.

However, progressive dispensationalism has rightly emphasized the overall, progressive outworking of God's redemptive plan for Jew and gentile in all its spiritual and physical/political dimensions. By refusing to separate off the millennium as a distinct entity but placing it within the larger historical, redemptive purposes of God, progressive dispensationalism's situating the millennium within the larger framework of the kingdom's "already" but "not-yet" aspects places it more within the mainstream of biblical scholarship. In this way, it is a distinct advance over its classical cousin.

4

Thematic Millennialism

—David L. Mathewson

Introduction

THE VIEW OF THE millennium discussed in this chapter cannot strictly be labeled premillennial if by "premillennial" we understand a strictly temporal sequence where the millennium is a transitional period of time of some length between this present age and the new heavens and new earth (Rev 21:1—22:5), a time period that occurs and extends *after* the second coming of Christ. However, we can probably include this view in our discussion of premillennialism because unlike other millennial views—amillennialism, postmillennialism—this view agrees with other premillennial views that the future second coming of Christ inaugurates the millennium; the thousand years does not take place sometime before it. However, unlike other premillennial schemes—classic and progressive dispensationalism, and historical premillennialism—this view does not necessarily postulate a period of time of some duration that temporally occurs in between (an *interregnum*) the second coming of Christ and the establishment of the new heavens and new earth (Revelation 21-22). This view of the millennium usually refrains from postulating a millennial period of any specific duration, and sees the main function of the millennium in Revelation 20 to symbolize important theological meanings such as judgment, vindication, and victory over Satan and death. The main point is not a distinct temporal phase between the present age and the consummated kingdom of the new creation. Rather the main point is the message and meaning that the millennium communicates. For lack of a better title, we have labeled this view "Thematic Millennialism," since the main focus of this view is the meanings or themes from Revelation that are encapsulated and symbolized in the reference to the thousand-year reign in Revelation 20. Some recent proponents of one form or another of this view of the millennium are Richard Bauckham, Gordon Fee, David Mathewson, Craig Koester, and R. J. McKelvey (see also J. Ramsey Michaels).[1] The following discussion will outline the main contours of this approach, beginning with the hermeneutical underpinnings.

Hermeneutical Considerations

This view of the millennium takes seriously (though this is not to suggest that other views do not) the literary genre of Revelation as apocalyptic and the function of Revelation 20:4–6 within the context of Revelation's final visionary segment (Rev 19:11—22:5). First, one of the distinct features of Revelation as belonging to the literary genre apocalypse is its preponderance of symbols. The primary medium of communication in Revelation is through symbol. What this means is that Revelation refers to reality, to real persons, places, and events, but it does so through the medium of symbols and images. There is no one-to-one correspondence between the symbol and the reality to which it refers. One only needs to compare the different depictions of Christ in Revelation 1:12–16; 5:6–7; 19:11–16, to be convinced that Revelation images reality rather than describing it "literally." John is referring to a real person (Christ), but is not describing him as one taking a photograph or video. The symbolism says something about who Christ is and what he does, rather than giving us a literal picture of what he looks like. Revelation itself

1. See their works cited below.

guides the reader in interpreting its language in 1:20, where the Son of Man interprets features of John's inaugural vision in 1:12–16: the seven stars refer to the angels of the seven churches, and the seven lampstands are the seven churches. What this means for this view of the millennium in Revelation 20:4–6 is that the reference to one thousand years does not need to, and probably is not intended to, describe an actual period of one thousand years duration. Instead, the interpreter should ask, what message is communicated by the image of the millennium? It conceivably could refer to a period of time much longer than a thousand years, or it could refer to a period of even much shorter duration, or not be concerned with a specific period of time at all.

This way of looking at the temporal designation "one thousand years" in Revelation 20:4–6 finds support in the fact that all the numbers, including the time periods, in Revelation are to be taken as symbolic as well: e.g., 4, 7, 12 and its multiples (e.g., 144,000), three-and-a-half years—forty-two months—1,260 days, 10 and its multiples. For example, the reference to three-and-a-half years (lit. "time, times, and half a time") says more about the *character* of the time of the churches struggle than it does the precise length of that period.[2] An example of the symbolic value of the time periods in Revelation can clearly be seen in 17:12: the allies of the beast "for *one hour* will receive authority as kings along with the beast." This does not mean that their reign only lasts for a literal sixty minutes (in fact, it would be difficult to conceive of how this could even happen); it simply means that their rule will be brief and limited.[3] Therefore, the interpreter cannot assume that the reference to a thousand years in Revelation 20:1–6 corresponds to a period of time of any specific duration. More important is the *meaning* communicated by the designation "one thousand years."

---

2. Most likely, the time periods three-and-a-half years, forty-two months, and 1,260 days refer to the entire period between the first and second coming of Christ. However, some would argue that it refers to a future, specific, and limited period of time immediately before the second coming of Christ.

3. Koester, *Revelation and the End of All Things*, 181.

A second important hermeneutical feature of this view of the millennium is that the literary context of the final visionary segment of Revelation (19:11—22:5) is paramount in understanding the role that the millennium plays in the final chapters, as well as in the entire book. Again, it is not that other views do not pay close attention to the literary context, but other premillennial views seem to place more stock in the overall theological underpinnings of the millennium in other OT and NT texts that refer to the establishment of the kingdom; that is, how does one assemble the pieces of the broader puzzle of OT texts which predict a coming kingdom, as well as their NT development, into a coherent millennial position (see classical and progressive dispensationalism)? For example, despite the fact that there is no reference to Israel's restoration to the land in Revelation 20:4–6, based on their understanding of OT prophecies and their relationship to the NT the millennium is where both classical and progressive dispensationalists, to varying degrees, find the promises of Israel's restoration and the establishment of an earthly kingdom fulfilled. It is not that these kinds of questions are ignored by the thematic view of the millennium, it is just that priority is given to the function of the millennium within the literary context and narrative of Revelation itself. That is, what role does the millennium seem to play within Revelation's *own* visionary structure? What connections does the millennium in Revelation 20:4–6 have with other sections of Revelation itself? What is the contribution of the millennium to John's own narrative?

It must be stressed that neither of the above two hermeneutical considerations requires that one will hold to this view of the millennium, nor are these observations unique to this approach. But they do play a crucial role in this interpretation of Revelation 20:4–6. So how specifically do those who hold to a more "thematic" view of the millennium understand the reference to the thousand years in Revelation 20:4–6?

Interpretation of Revelation 20

Revelation 20:4–6

As already noted, this thematic view of the millennium focuses on the meaning of the symbol of the thousand years in Revelation 20:4–6. Rather than seeing it as a distinct period of time of some duration, this view considers the role the millennium plays within the wider literary context of Revelation, and what themes or meanings are communicated by the image of the saints coming to life and reigning with Christ for a thousand years. The following discussion will begin broadly with recognized connections between Revelation 20:4–6 and the rest of the book, narrowing the focus to the context and interpretation of Revelation 20 itself.

The Broader Context of Revelation

For those who hold to this view of the millennium, the event that transpires in Revelation 20:4–6 is already anticipated in other sections of Revelation. In the messages to the seven churches (chaps. 2–3), those who overcome are promised exemption from the second death (2:11). In 20:4–6, those who have overcome through martyrdom are now given life, and escape the second death (20:14). Moreover, those who overcome have authority over all nations and rule with Christ (2:26–27), sitting on his throne (3:21). The reference to the millennium should also be seen as a response to the fifth seal in 6:10. "The martyrs died 'for their testimony to Jesus and for the word of God' (20:4) and their vindication is the answer to the question of theodicy posed by their deaths (6:10)."[4] The description of the saints in both texts as "beheaded/slaughtered for the testimony of Jesus and the word of God" (6:9; 20:4) ties the two sections together. Therefore, whatever else the millennium does in Revelation, it functions as the vindication of the suffering people of God, particularly *the reward for the martyrs* who die for the testimony of

---

4. McKelvey, "The Millennium and the Second Coming," 97.

Jesus. Mounce appropriately concludes that the millennium is "a special reward to the martyrs of chapter 6."[5]

This view also interprets the reference to the one thousand years in relationship to the other time periods in the book of Revelation, periods that describe this present age of the church's struggle with evil, the dragon, and the two beasts. Most of these time references are found in chapters 11–13. There are three important time references in these chapters: three-and-a-half years (time, times, half a time), forty-two months, 1,260 days (11:2, 3; 12:6, 14; 13:5). All of these are used to depict the time when Satan and his two beastly cohorts wreak havoc on the people of God, the church. Most would understand these temporal designations are referring to the entire period between the first and second coming of Christ, though some would reserve it for a specific period just prior to the second coming of Christ (the great tribulation). No matter which view one takes, all three of these time designations refer to 1) the *same* period of time, from different perspectives; 2) a *limited* period of time (in 12:12 it is designated as a "short time"); 3) focus more on the *character* of the time of the churches struggle rather than the length of time (an intense period of persecution, a time of testing, but a time that will not last forever; it is limited). The important point for this view of the millennium is that the symbolic value of one thousand years stands in *contrast* to these other designations of the time of Satan and the beasts: the thousand years is a much *longer* period of time in comparison; i.e., three-and-a-half years, forty-two months, and 1,260 days are rather brief and insignificant in comparison to one thousand years. Satan's reign in 12:10 is characterized as only for a "short time" (*holigon kairon*). The point of the contrast, then, is not how long these two periods of time will last (the churches struggle, the millennium), but *the meaning* that the temporal designations communicate: the period of suffering is insignificant compared to the millennium. The millennium will far exceed and more than compensate for the period of suffering under Satan and the beast.

---

5. Mounce, *Revelation*, 359.

In Revelation 12–13, the dragon (Satan) and the two beasts are depicted as making war with the saints. The identical reference to the dragon, the serpent from Genesis 3, in Revelation 12:9 and 20:1 ties the two sections together. This means that at one level the millennium in 20:4–6 is to be seen as a counterpart to the events in chapters 12–13. In these chapters the dragon and the beasts rule over the earth, and they make war with the saints, who resist and contest their rule. The dragon puts them to death. In 12:10, Satan is described as the accuser of our brothers and sisters, the one accusing them before the throne day and night. Now in a profound reversal Satan is judged and the saints come to life and reign in 20:4–6. In chapters 12–13, the saints "contested the Beast's right to rule and paid the price for doing so, and now they share Christ's victory and reign."[6]

Mathewson also argues that a parallel to Revelation 20:4–6 can be found in 11:11–13.[7] After the ministry of the two witnesses, who are put to death in apparent defeat, they are brought to life and taken up to heaven in 11:11. Then comes the end-time judgment in vv. 12–13. Verse 11 clearly portrays the resurrection of the two witnesses (which symbolize the entire witnessing church) at the end of history. The point is that God raises his two witnesses who were put to death by the beast in order to vindicate them before the eyes of the world. This is precisely the event portrayed in 20:4–6, but now symbolized by one thousand years. A further parallel can be found in the seventh trumpet in 11:18. In this verse, the song of the twenty-four elders announces that "the time has come for the dead to be judged, and to give the servants and prophets and the saints and all those who fear your name their reward . . . and to destroy those who destroy the earth." This corresponds roughly in reverse order to the main themes articulated in 19:11—20:15: the judgment of the dead (20:11–15); the reward of the saints (20:4–6); and the destruction of those who destroy the earth (19:11–21; 20:7–10). The millennium is an extension of the seventh trumpet,

---

6. McKelvey, "Millennium and Second Coming," 97.
7. Mathewson, "Re-examination of the Millennium," 245–46.

which occurs at the parousia.[8] Although it does not rule out an additional reign of some length that occurs between the second coming of Christ and the new heavens and new earth, it should be noted that there are no references elsewhere in Revelation to such an interregnum when Revelation envisions the establishment of God's kingdom—it appears that only the final form of the kingdom occurs when "The kingdom of the world has become the kingdom of our Lord and his Christ, and he will reign forever and ever" (11:15). It is at *this* time that the saints will be rewarded for their faithful witness, symbolized by the millennial reign.

Revelation 19:11—22:5

One's view of the millennium depends much on how the interpreter relates the different parts of this section (19:11—22:5) to each other. Do the various segments of the vision indicated a sequence of events? Or are they simply different images that depict different effects of the coming of Christ at the end of history? Along with other premillennial views, the thematic millennial view sees all the events beginning with 19:11 as depicting a complex of events that transpire at or as a result of the second coming of Christ. What we are calling a thematic view of the millennium focuses on the role that the millennium plays within this sequence of visions in 19:11—20:15. However, it does not necessarily see a *temporal* sequence of events in this section. That is, unlike other millennial views (dispensational and historical), a thematic view of the millennium does not see it as a temporal period that extends between (a) the second coming of Christ (19:11–21) and (b) the final judgment and the new heavens and new earth (20:11—22:5). In fact, all throughout Revelation the repeated phrase "And I saw" (*kai eidon*) need only refer to the sequence in which John *saw* the visions, not the temporal sequence in which they will *occur* (though there is a temporal progression from judgment [19:11—20:15] to the establishment of the new creation [21:1—22:5]). The thematic

---

8. Mathewson, "Reexamination of the Millennium," 243. See Bauckham, *Climax of Prophecy*, 21.

view of the millennium, then, does not see the reference to a thousand years as depicting a literal period of time that temporally comes between the coming of Christ and the arrival of the new creation. According to Fee, "John is not at this point interested in a time period as such."[9] Many conceptions of the millennium are "based on the mistaken view that John's millennium is to be taken literally."[10] 19:11—20:15 depict a series of removal scenes, or judgment scenes, which transpire at the second coming of Christ, with two battle scenes (19:11–21; 20:7–10) and a final great white throne judgment (20:11–15).

Mathewson argues that there is recapitulation of visions (the two battle scenes in 19:11–21; 20:7–10), but *within* the reference to the second coming.[11] The entire section 19:11—20:15 constitutes a series of visions that depict the *same* reality: what will happen at the second coming of Christ. It does not necessarily provide a chronological sequence of events that will transpire after the second coming of Christ; it is arranged *thematically*, to emphasize the meaning of Christ's coming to bring judgment. Fee argues that 20:1–6 is an interlude in between two descriptions of the end time battle narrated in 19:11–21 and 20:7–10. The meaning of the millennium is to be understood in terms of the role that it plays within this context. The judgment of the two beasts (19:11–21) and Satan (20:1–3, 7–11) requires the positive corollary of the vindication and reward of those who have been put to death at the hands of this evil triumvirate. Thus, "for John true justice involves more than actions *against* the perpetrators of evil; it means acting *for* the well-being of those who have suffered."[12] According to Koester, "The martyrs asked for justice in 6:10, and God acted in their favor with his negative judgment against Babylon and the beast (18:8, 20; 19:2, 11) [and we would add, against the dragon, Satan (20:1–3, 7–10)]. Now God's positive judgment is evident in the martyrs' resurrection to life in Christ's kingdom

---

9. Fee, *Revelation*, 280.
10. McKelvey, "The Millennium," 98.
11. Mathewson, "A Re-examination of the Millennium," 238–42.
12. Koester, *Revelation*, 785.

(20:4)."[13] Thus, the dative case of the personal pronoun *autois* in 20:4a should be understood in terms of "judgment was given for them," or "they were given a favorable verdict,"[14] rather than them being given a role of judging. This is the role that the millennium plays in 20:4–6. It is not so much intended to provide a literal piece of temporal information, but is *a symbolic way of depicting the vindication of the saints in the context of the judgment of those who ruled over them and put them to death*: now they come to life and reign. According to Bauckham, "the negative aspect of the final judgment (19:11–21), in which the beast was condemned, requires as it positive counterpart that judgment be given in favor of the martyrs, who must be vindicated and rewarded."[15] Thus, this view of the millennium refrains from reading a temporal meaning into the reference to the thousand years, and focuses instead on the meaning communicated by the symbol (see below).

The Context of Revelation 20

The thematic view of the millennium would rely on many of the same arguments as other premillennial views to show that the millennium transpires at the second coming of Christ: the absolute binding of Satan in 20:1–3; the reference to the two physical resurrections in 20:4–6, 11–15. As already seen above, John appears to see the millennium as an extension of the seventh trumpet (see 11:18), which occurs at the coming of Christ at the end of history. However, according to a thematic view of the millennium, within the context that John gives it, the millennium is not meant to designate a specific period of time, but is a metaphorical means of indicating the vindication and triumph of the saints who have died for their testimony for Jesus. Within the context of the overall narrative of 19:11—20:15, it portrays a further effect of the parousia of Christ (his second coming). According to Mathewson,

---

13. Koester, *Revelation*, 772.
14. See Mathewson, *Revelation*, 274–75 for discussion.
15. Bauckham, *Theology*, 107.

"the reference to the one thousand years is important, not for the temporal information it conveys, but for its *meaning* and *thematic* value: it metaphorically portrays the complete victory and vindication of the saints at the parousia of Christ."[16] Mounce seems to say something similar when he distinguishes between the form (a one-thousand-year reign) and the essential truth (vindication of the martyrs) of Revelation 20:4–6.[17] "One thousand is a round number that indicated completeness and, as ten cubed [10 × 10 × 10], symmetry."[18] The number one thousand is symbolic of the *complete* and *total* vindication and triumph. It indicates "fullness"[19] or "vastness."[20] As seen above, it contrasts with the shorter periods of time used to depict the rule of the dragon and the beasts, who persecuted and put to death God's people: three-and-a-half years, forty-two months, 1,260 days (also symbolic in value), the "short time" of the already-defeated dragon's activity. Now the vindication of the saints more than compensates for anything they suffered under Satan and the beast.

The reference to the millennium in 20:4–6 occurs in between the two-stage defeat of Satan in 20:1–3, 7–10: first he is bound, and then he is released to gather an army for one last-ditch effort to destroy God's people, which results in his resounding defeat. Again, more important than trying to make temporal sense of this (such as asking where the people came from who populate the millennium and who make up the army), the interpreter should ask what *meaning* the imagery conveys. Scholars who hold this view of the millennium provide different (though complementary) explanations for this textual phenomenon. According to Fee, "sitting as it does between the two parts of the Last Battle, its overall intent appears to be a final word of comfort to those who are yet to be martyred for their devotion to Christ rather than offering unqualified

---

16. Mathewson, "Re-examination of the Millennium," 248. Italics his.
17. Mounce, *Revelation*, 359.
18. Koester, *Revelation*, 773.
19. Koester, *End of All Things*, 183.
20. Koester, *Revelation*, 773.

allegiance to the emperor."[21] That is, the "this thousand-year hiatus assure[s] the martyrs that they are not forgotten in the divine scheme of things."[22] Bauckham asserts that "to demonstrate that their triumph in Christ's kingdom is not one which evil can again reverse, that it is God's last word for good against evil, the devil is given a last chance to deceive the nations again (20:7–8)."[23] And McKelvey summarizes that "John's account of the release of Satan and the resumption of the holy war points to the resilience of evil and its immeasurable capacity to create trouble and thus reminds his readers that they never cease to depend upon divine assistance. But John is equally concerned to show that the battle between good and evil does not last forever. God is sovereign."[24] The two-fold judgment of Satan may also reflect that way that satanic or demonic figures are disposed of in apocalyptic literature: imprisonment, followed by release and final judgment (see Isa 24:21–22; 1 Enoch 10:4–6, 11–13; 53:3–5; 54:1–6; 2 Pet 2:4; Jude 6).[25] Again, the point is not to narrative a temporal sequence, but to communicate important themes.

Textually, there is no clear mention of *where* the millennium takes place in 20:4–6. Is it in heaven, or on earth? John's cryptic reference makes no clear mention of this, so that the reign of the saints with Christ could take place on earth or in heaven, and so some are understandably hesitant to drawn any specific conclusions as to its location.[26] However, Fee and McKelvey think that it must take place on earth.[27] McKelvey concludes that the implication is that the millennium takes place on earth: "Throughout

---

21. Fee, *Revelation*, 280.
22. Fee, *Revelation*, 280.
23. Bauckham, *Revelation*, 107.
24. McKelvey, "Millennium and Second Coming," 98–99.
25. Mathewson, Re-examination of the Millennium," 249.
26. Mathewson, Re-examination of the Millennium," 251; Koester, *End of All Things*, 184–85. See Morris, *Revelation*, 228.
27. McKelvey, "Millennium and Second Coming," 97–98; Fee, *Revelation*, 282: "And even though there is no specific geographical location given, John seems clearly to have planet earth still in view."

Revelation the earth is the place where God's sovereignty is challenged and suffering is caused to the followers of the Lamb and countless others (18:24). It is on earth, therefore, that God will vindicate his sovereignty and champion the cause of all those who suffer unjustly."[28] Yet Fee and McKelvey refuse to speculate as to *what* happens on earth, and stop far short of dispensational and historical premillennial schemes (e.g., the time and place when Israel's promises are fulfilled for dispensational approaches; or a period of time with unprecedented peace and righteousness on earth; or questions about pro-creation or how resurrected and unresurrected people can coexist in the millennial period).

The Meaning of the Millennium

Given the discussion above concerning the role of Revelation 20:4–6 in its broader context, the context of 19:11—20:14, and the details of Revelation 20:1–6 itself, what is the overall *meaning(s)* communicated by the reference to the so-called millennium in Revelation 20:4–6? As already seen with scholars who hold this view, the teaching concerning the thousand years is not to be interpreted literally, and so it does not depict a literal temporal period. What is important is not the temporal information that it provides. What is important is the *role* that John gives it in his own vision and the *meaning* communicated by the metaphor of the thousand years.[29] Rudolph Schnackenburg concludes that "the vision is a symbolical description of the martyrs' victory and their special, appropriate reward."[30] According to Bauckham, "the theological point of the millennium is solely to demonstrate the triumph of the martyrs: that those whom the beast put to death are those who will truly live—eschatologically, and that those who contested his right to rule and suffered for it are those who in the end rule

---

28. McKelvey, "Millennium and Second Coming," 98.

29. McKelvey states bluntly, "The millennium is a metaphor" ("Millennium and Second Coming," 98).

30. Schnackenburg, *God's Rule and Kingdom*, 346.

as universally as he—and for much longer: a thousand years!"[31] Therefore, "John expected the martyrs to be vindicated, but the millennium depicts the meaning, rather than predicting the manner of their vindication."[32] Likewise, Fee says that the millennium indicates that the martyrs have a special place in God's plan, that God has not forgotten them in the midst of their struggle with the state.[33] The image of the millennium demonstrates the triumph and vindication of the martyrs who were put to death under the reign of the dragon and the beast. Now in a profound reversal they come to life and reign with Christ.[34] That is, the millennium should be understood "as symbolically portraying the vindication and triumph of the saints as the positive correlation to the judgment at the second coming."[35] The millennium means the vindication of God's sovereignty and those who have suffered unjustly, and the triumph over evil and injustice.[36] To summarize, according to this view, John sees in his vision the saints coming to life and reigning for a period of one thousand years. But what this scene refers to is summarized by the meanings pointed out above.

Conclusion

When examined in light of the literary context of Revelation, the millennium plays a specific role within John's visionary narrative. According to those who hold to this view of the millennium, the one thousand years symbolically depicts the ultimate victory and vindication of the saints who suffered for their faithful witness to

---

31. Bauckham, *Theology*, 107. See also Ramsey Michaels, *Interpreting Revelation*, 146: "Its [the millennium's] theological contributions to the Book of Revelation are its graphic pictures of the vindication of the martyrs and of Satan's final consignment to the lake of fire."

32. Bauckham, *Theology*, 108.

33. Fee, *Revelation*, 281–82.

34. Bauckham, *Theology*, 107; Mathewson, "Re-examination of the Millennium," 249–50.

35. Mathewson, "Reexamination of the Millennium," 250.

36. McKelvey, "Millennium and Second Coming," 98.

Christ. This means that the millennium is *not* to be seen as a temporal period that forms a transition time of some length between this present age and the new creation in Revelation 21:1—22:5. Furthermore, this also means that the millennium probably should not be assigned the importance that has been given it throughout church history, for example, when our eschatology is categorized according to whether it is premillennial, amillennial, or postmillennial; or our interpretations of Revelation are identified according to how they treat the millennium in Revelation 20:4-6 (e.g., a premillennial reading of Revelation, or an amillennial reading of Revelation). Pride of place, according to the symbolic view, goes to the new heavens and new earth of Revelation 21:1—22:5. J. Ramsey Michaels comments that "John's interest in it [the millennium] is not for its own sake but as a kind of threshold to his visions of the new world and its new holy city (chaps. 21–22)."[37] In fact, this final vision of the new creation and new Jerusalem is where all the OT texts concerning Israel's restoration on earth are found alluded to.[38] Koester comments that

> Revelation itself does not associate any of these Old Testament passages [e.g., Isaiah 65] with the millennial kingdom. John will make lavish use of Old Testament passages when describing the New Jerusalem in Rev. 21:1—22:5. . . . . He describes the thousand-year reign of the saints in remarkable sparse prose, without the allusions to the Old Testament texts that he includes so freely in other visions.[39]

Similarly, Mounce suggests that "The millennium is not, for John, the messianic age foretold by the prophets of the OT, but a special reward for those who have paid with their lives the price of faithful opposition to the idolatrous claims of Antichrist."[40] Unless one insists on significant or complete discontinuity between this present earth and the new creation, there is no need to insist on

---

37. Michaels, *Revelation*, 146.
38. Mathewson, *New Heaven and a New Earth*.
39. Koester, *End of All Things*, 183–84. So also Mounce, *Revelation*, 359.
40. Mounce, *Revelation*, 359.

a fulfillment of the OT prophetic texts on this present earth, as if God's purposes can only be vindicated in the form of this present earth. The new creation of Revelation 21:1—22:5 *is* this earth, renewed, restored, and vindicated. To find in 20:4–6 a restoration of Israel, a renewal of the earth, etc., reads into the millennium more than the role that John himself gives to the millennium.

Although apocalyptic texts sometimes depict a temporary, earthly kingdom before the consummation of all things (1 Enoch 93:3–17; 4 Ezra 7:26–44; 12:31–34; 2 Baruch 29:3—30:1; 40:1–4; 72:2—73:3), this does not necessarily mean that John also expects a similar time period, one that he designates as a thousand years. If John is dependent on the notion of the temporary kingdom from apocalyptic texts (and not all who hold this view are convinced that he is), he has certainly given it its own function within his visionary narrative. For the thematic view of the millennium, Revelation 20:4–6 is not the temporary messianic kingdom promised in the OT or found in the above apocalyptic texts. Once more, those who hold to this view limit the purpose of the millennium to the role that John himself gives it in Revelation, not as referring to a literal period of time, but as symbolizing vindication, reward, and triumph, in the context of the judgment of Satan and the beasts.

Critical Engagement

The thematic view of the millennium is to be applauded especially for its focus on the function of the millennium within the narrative of Revelation. It focuses primarily on the meaning and thematics of the millennium in Revelation 20:4–6. It also takes seriously the nature of symbolism as applied to John's language of one thousand years. This view of the millennium is primarily interested in the role that the millennium plays in Revelation itself, rather than seeing it as the place where Old Testament promises of an earthly kingdom with restored Israel and redeemed nations living in a time of unparalleled peace and prosperity converge and will be fulfilled. This view refuses to speculate as to what will take place in the millennial kingdom, beyond the reference to the saints coming to life and reigning. In this way it is tied very closely to the literary context of Revelation itself and the relationship of Revelation 20 to its broader context. Such a view of the millennium relieves the interpreter of the need to deal with problems other views create—who populates the millennium after the judgment in 19:11–21? How do we account for both resurrected and non-resurrected people in millennium? Where do the people come from for the final battle in 20:7–10? But if the millennium is not a reference to a period of time, then problems such as this quickly dissolve.

Furthermore, this view of millennium also places the focus where John himself seems to place it—on the new creation, not on millennium. The new creation and new Jerusalem in 21:1—22:5 are the "grand finale" so to speak, the final goal of creation. Thus, textually it occupies a more significant amount of space in John's narrative, as well as containing a much louder volume of OT allusions. As seen above, this is where all the OT prophetic texts promising restoration emerge in bold color. The new creation is the climax of God's promises and his purposes for humanity and creation, not the millennium.

However, for some this view of the millennium may too quickly gloss over the apparent temporal language in chapter 20. Specifically, there seems to be a sequence suggested with Satan's binding in the abyss (20:1–3), then his release and final battle/defeat (20:7–11), separated by a period of one thousand years (20:4–6). Also, there appears to be a separation of two resurrections, one at the start of the one thousand years and another one after (20:11–15). This does not require that the interpreter takes the thousand years as literal calendar years, but it does seem to suggest for some a period of time of some duration (the one thousand years could simply symbolize a long, ideal period of time) between the two resurrections (20:4–6, 11–15) and the two battles (19:11–21; 20:7–10).

Furthermore, this view also seems to ignore the role that the millennium has played throughout church history. The millennium has played an important role throughout the reception history of Revelation in the church and sometimes has had important ramifications politically and theologically.[41] It has often served to summarize various approaches to the book of Revelation (e.g., a premillennial interpretation of Revelation). To suggest that the millennium plays a less important role in Revelation or that it does not refer to a specific period of time may too quickly ignore large segments of church history which have found in the millennium a key feature of their eschatological thinking. Moreover, for the most part this view of the millennium is fairly recent, and finds minimal support historically in the church's understanding of the millennium.[42] This does not mean that the thematic view of the millennium is incorrect, but we must bear in mind that views that have little precedent in the collective wisdom of the church must be approached with caution.

---

41. See Wainwright, *Mysterious Apocalypse*, 21-87 for a brief history of interpreting the millennium.

42. A possible precursor of a view of the millennium that does not see it as a period of time of some length can be found in Hippolytus, *Chapters against Gaius*, based on the observation that a day is as a thousand years to the Lord (Ps 90:4). In Britain Joseph Mede (1586-1638) followed a similar approach. A day is as a thousand years to God, so the millennium will be a day of judgment (*Works*, 2 vols [London: James Flesher, 1664], 2:747-51).

5

Historic Premillennialism in South Korea

—Sung Wook Chung

Introduction

IN THIS CHAPTER, WE will discuss historic premillennialism beyond the Western context, specifically in the Asian context of South Korea. It is hard to know precisely how historic premillennialism is viewed, accepted, and developed in some Asian countries. There are some prominent historical premillennialists, such as the Chinese Singaporean scholar Tony Siew, who actively teaches and spreads the historic premillennial view. Siew has long served as lecturer of New Testament at Trinity Theological College in Singapore, and his book *The War between the Two Beasts and the Two Witnesses: A Chiastic Reading of Revelation 11:1—14:5* espouses the historic premillennial view of biblical eschatology. However, it is in South Korea that historic premillennialism has been flourishing and advancing more than any other country in Asia. Thus, this chapter will focus on the historical development and features of historic premillennialism in the Korean context, focusing on its major advocates and their arguments.

Historical Development and Major Advocates of Historic Premillennialism in South Korea

There were both historic premillennialists and dispensationalists among the first Western missionaries to Korea in the late nineteenth century. Interestingly, very few of these missionaries were amillennial. Through the influence of the first missionaries, historic premillennialism became the dominant view during the inception and the early stages of the Korean church. In addition, subsequently many of Korea's native theologians have held to the historic premillennial view.

For example, Dr. Hyung Ryong Park (1897–1978), who is regarded as the father of Korean Reformed theology, became a historic premillennialist through his studies at American institutions such as Princeton Theological Seminary and Southern Baptist Theological Seminary. Dr. Yoon Sun Park (1905–88), an exegetical scholar, also became a historic premillennialist through his education at Westminster Theological Seminary in Philadelphia and the Free University of Amsterdam in the Netherlands. If it was Hyung Ryong Park who established Presbyterian systematic theology in Korea, it was Yoon Sun Park who established Protestant exegetical theology in Korea. Yoon Sun Park, along with Sang Geun Lee, was the representative exegetical theologian of the Korean church. From 1934 to 1936, he studied at Westminster Theological Seminary, where he was deeply influenced by J. Gresham Machen. From 1938 to 1939, he studied Christian apologetics at Westminster under Cornelius Van Til. Then, from 1953 to 1954, he studied at the Free University of Amsterdam. Interestingly, he rejected the amillennial view despite having studied at Westminster and the Free University, both schools where amillennialism was prevalent. In 1979, he completed his commentary on the entirety of the Old and New Testaments. Yoon Sun Park taught in Korean seminaries for several decades, disseminating the historic premillennial view and raising many disciples as scholars and ministers. His commentary is widely read, and this alone shows that, like Hyung Ryong Park, Yoon Sun Park made a tremendous contribution to furthering historic premillennialism in Korea. These two figures taught numerous students the historic view of the millennium. As a result, it became popular among pastors of local churches in Korea.

This, however, changed in the 1960s, '70s, and '80s when Pentecostalism swept the nation with a revival movement and David Yonggi Cho and the famous Yoido Full Gospel Church stood in the center of that movement. With Pentecostalism came dispensationalism, with Cho as one of its most outspoken advocates.

Then, in the 1990s, many Korean biblical scholars who were trained in Europe and the United States returned to Korea and introduced amillennialism to the country. As a result, amillennialism started gaining popularity among Korean pastors and scholars and continues to do so, even today. Notable amillennialists include Sung Soo Kwon, Pil Chan Lee, and Kap Jong Choi.

Dispensationalism continues to have the greatest influence among the lay Christians in Korea, and it is only recently through the efforts of seminary professors such as Soo Am Park and Jung Gun Han and local pastors such as Hyung Tae Kim, Byeong Seok Min, and Gwang Bok Lee that historic premillennialism is starting to gain favor again among pastors and church parishioners. We shall consider their work briefly.

Soo Am Park (1940–) graduated from Keimyung University and Kyungpook National University. Afterward, he completed his MDiv at Presbyterian University and Theological Seminary of Korea, finished the ThM degree at Western Theological Seminary in Michigan, and earned his PhD at Knox College at the University of Toronto in Canada. He then returned to his alma mater, Presbyterian University and Theological Seminary, to teach biblical theology. After retirement, he held office as President of Presbyterian Theological Seminary in Moscow, Russia. With respect to eschatology, he actively supported the historic premillennial view. His book *Revelation: New Testament Commentary* embraced historic premillennialism and interpreted Revelation from that perspective.

Jung Gun Han (1949–) graduated from Joong Ang University and Korea Theological Seminary. He then went to Biblical

Theological Seminary in Pennsylvania to study Old Testament theology. There he completed his STM and then went on to Potchefstroom University of South Africa to finish his doctoral degree in Old Testament theology. Returning to Korea, he taught Old Testament theology at his alma mater Korea Theological Seminary. Since 2009 he has been serving as the Dean of the Graduate School of Korea Theological Seminary. Throughout his career, Han demonstrated a special interest in biblical eschatology and actively supported historic premillennialism. Through books such as *Biblical Illumination of Eschatology Today*, *Revelation Commentary*, and *Introduction to Eschatology*, Han actively supported the historic premillennial perspective. He also wrote various journal articles expounding on the biblical soundness and the hermeneutical verity of historic premillennialism.

Hyung Ryong Park (1897–1978): The Father of Historic Premillennialism in Korea

Hyung Ryong Park, also known as the father of Reformed theology in Korea, moved to the United States in 1921 and received the ThM degree at Princeton Theological Seminary two years later. He later finished his doctoral degree at Southern Baptist Theological Seminary in Louisville, Kentucky. Hyung Ryong Park embraced Puritan Reformed theology as his own and spread the historic premillennial view through his seven-volume masterpiece *Dogmatics* (1964–73). It is not clear how he came to adopt historic premillennialism, but one can carefully speculate that Park did so during his studies at Princeton between 1921 and 1923. This was at a time when Charles R. Erdman (1866–1960) was teaching practical theology there. Considering the fact that Erdman strongly advocated the historic premillennial view, we can imagine what influence he and the school might have had on Park.

Teaching in Korean seminaries for many decades, Park further advanced the historic premillennial view, which he believed to be the most faithful among millennial views to biblical eschatological teaching. Countless numbers of his disciples read his *Dogmatics* and applied it to their ministries. This alone shows how great a contribution Park made in spreading historic premillennialism in Korea.

Eschatological Framework

In order to examine Park's eschatology, I will analyze his *Doctrine of the Next World*, the seventh volume of his *Dogmatics*. Park's eschatological framework is basically historic premillennialist and posttribulational. His approach to the interpretation of the book of Revelation is considerably futuristic. He believes that the church will go through the great tribulation and will be transformed and raptured at the end of that tribulation when the Lord returns. At the same time, the righteous dead will be resurrected. After welcoming the Lord in the sky, the resurrected and transformed will come down to the earth and enter into the millennial kingdom to reign with the Lord Jesus. At the end of the millennium, Satan will be released and deceive Gog and Magog to rebel against God, and they will be completely destroyed. And then all the unrighteous dead will be resurrected to be judged at the great white throne together with Satan, death, and Hades.

The Second Coming of Christ

In addition to this broad eschatological framework, Park discusses the second coming of Christ, delving into its reality and importance. For Park, the second coming of Christ will be factual primarily because Scripture confirms it. After raising the question of why the doctrine of the second coming of Christ is important, he presents several answers. First, it is important because it has a paramount position in Scripture. Second, the Lord's second coming is key to an appropriate understanding of the whole of Scripture. Third, the parousia is the blessed hope of the church. Fourth, the second coming of the Lord is the catalyst for biblical Christianity. Fifth, the Lord's second coming is a significant impetus for Christian service. Finally, it is the culmination of the summation of the Christian faith.[1]

Great Events Before the Second Coming of the Lord

After discussing the factuality and importance of the Lord's second coming, Park discusses the great events or signs of the second coming. Park argues that the first event is the preaching of the gospel all over the world, referring to Matthew 24:14, Mark 13:10, and Romans 11:25. This will occur in the church age and will be fulfilled through the conversions of numerous Gentiles. Second, national Israel will convert to Christ. Taking Romans 11:26 rather literally, Park argues that at the end of the church age and right before the Lord's second coming, national Israel will convert to the gospel collectively. Third, he argues that the Lord Jesus taught that the great apostasy would occur before his second coming, appealing to Matthew 24:9–12, Mark 13:9–22, and Luke 21:22–24. For Park, the apostle Paul also taught about the great apostasy (2 Thess 2:3; 1 Tim 4:1; and 2 Tim 3:1–5). Fourth, there will be the great tribulation before the Lord's second coming. According to Park, Jesus taught about this in Matthew 24:21–24 and Luke 21:20–28.[2]

Fifth, the Antichrist will appear right before the Lord's second coming. For Park, the Antichrist will be a single person who will rebel against God and persecute the church as a global dictator.[3] Finally, Park argues that there will be many signs and wonders before the Lord's second coming.[4] It is important to note here that as a historic premillennialist Park pays keen and detailed attention to the events and signs prior to the parousia, while contemporary Western historic premillennialists have demonstrated tendencies to disregard these signs and events. This reflects a distinctive

---

1. Park, *Doctrine of the Next World*, 175–84.
2. Park, *Doctrine of the Next World*, 184–89.
3. Park, *Doctrine of the Next World*, 190–97.
4. Park, *Doctrine of the Next World*, 197–98.

tendency among historic premillennialists in South Korea in contrast to Western historic premillennialists

Two Resurrections

In relation to the subject of the resurrection, Park seems to agree with traditional historic premillennialists that there will be two resurrections. Park interprets the first resurrection in Revelation 20:4–6 to be the resurrection of the righteous dead. Thus, all of the believers who are already dead will participate in the first resurrection. He does not consider the first resurrection as the resurrection of martyrs alone. For Park, following the millennial kingdom, the unrighteous dead will be raised again to face the judgment at the great white throne.[5] He appeals to 1 Corinthians 15:22–24, interpreting v. 24 to mean that the final resurrection will be for the *unrighteous* dead alone. As we will explore later, Byeong Seok Min rebutted such an interpretation, arguing that the first resurrection will be for martyrs alone and that both the unrighteous dead *and* the righteous dead will participate in the resurrection following the millennial kingdom.

The Millennial Kingdom

Park discusses a variety of approaches to the millennial kingdom, including amillennialism, postmillennialism, historic premillennialism, and dispensational premillennialism. He definitely believes that historic premillennialism is the best option, being the one he judges most consistent with Scripture. In terms of his discussion of the millennial kingdom, Park basically concurs with major Western historic premillennialists, especially Charles R. Erdman and George E. Ladd (1911–82).

According to Park, right after the Lord's return the Lord Jesus will establish the millennial kingdom on earth. The city of Jerusalem will be rebuilt and numerous gentiles will enter into that

---

5. Park, *Doctrine of the Next World*, 303–8.

kingdom. The Lord will reign gloriously in the millennial kingdom, and the resurrected and transformed believers will participate in his reign. National Israel will convert to Christ and they will preach the gospel to the gentiles during the millennium. Peace and righteousness will fill the millennium, and the earth will produce abundant fruits and grains. Even unbelieving gentiles, not yet resurrected and transformed, will enjoy long and comfortable life.[6]

Who will reproduce in the millennial kingdom? Park seems to agree with Ladd and other traditional historic premillennialists that unbelieving gentiles will reproduce many offspring and that some of them will rebel against God as Gog and Magog. He also argues that the millennium will not be an absolutely perfect world; rather, it will be like the Garden of Eden before the fall.[7]

Hyung Tae Kim (1930–2006)

At the age of eighteen, Hyung Tae Kim defected from Pyongyang, North Korea, to Seoul. He graduated from Central Theological University and continued his studies at Presbyterian University and Theological Seminary. Afterward, he received his Doctor of Divinity degree and served as the moderator of the Yongchun Presbytery of the Presbyterian Church of Korea. He was a regular speaker at the Sion World Mission Church in New York, and he led leadership conferences and revivals in New York for a total of fifty-one times. He also led a total of 101 leadership conferences and revivals in Korea as director of Seongsan monastery in Korea. He started traveling worldwide in 1988, and as a traveling evangelist for over fifty years, he taught church leaders in Russia, Pakistan, and Thailand, among other countries. Kim also served as senior pastor of Sion Church for twenty-two years (1978–2000). For over thirty years, he led leadership conferences and revivals specifically geared toward pastors and ministers. Through these domestic and foreign speaking engagements, Kim contributed greatly to the

---

6. Park, *Doctrine of the Next World*, 271.
7. Park, *Doctrine of the Next World*, 276–77.

furthering of the doctrine of historic premillennialism. He is especially known for interpreting the end-time signs. His books *Prophesy against Gog, People after the Word of God, Will You Restore Me at This Time?, God's Gospel, What Must Take Place after This,* and *Shining Lampstand of Gold* are some of his most well-known in this regard. Although he did not have academic training in theological research, he had tremendous influence as a public speaker, author, and pastor. He was able to disseminate the historic premillennial view among both pastors and lay believers worldwide. Kim emphasized the signs of the second coming, taught that the church will undergo the trials of the great tribulation, and affirmed the reality of the earthly millennial kingdom. He believed, taught, and ministered with deeply historic premillennial convictions.

Eschatological Framework

Hyung Tae Kim's eschatological framework is consistent with historic premillennialism. According to Kim, the church will undergo the great tribulation and the Lord will come again at the end of that tribulation. When the Lord does so, the first resurrection of the righteous dead and the transformation of believers will occur. After the parousia, the Lord Jesus will establish and rule over the millennial kingdom on earth. At the end of the millennial kingdom, Satan will be released and will attempt to deceive Gog and Magog, but he will be thrown into the lake of fire. At the great white throne, the second resurrection of the unrighteous dead will occur. After the judgment that will occur there, the eternal kingdom of God will be established in the new heaven and new earth. In sum, Kim's eschatological framework is similar to that of traditional historic premillennialism.

Covenantal Hermeneutics and the Kingdom of God

In his eschatological preaching and writing, Kim employed covenantal hermeneutics to interpret Scripture and emphasized the kingdom of God as the central theme of the entire Bible. Overall, his covenantal hermeneutics is consistent with traditional Reformed covenant theology, which was first championed by seventeenth-century Reformed orthodox theologians such as Thomas Goodwin (1600–1680), John Owen (1616–83), Johannes Cocceius (1603–69), and Hermann Witsius (1633–1708). Traditional Reformed covenant theology is characterized by its threefold covenantal scheme of the covenant of redemption, the covenant of works, and the covenant of grace. It seems that Kim accepted this basic framework.

However, it is important to appreciate that Kim goes beyond traditional Reformed covenantal theology by arguing that Scripture presents a covenant of the kingdom or a covenant of blessing prior to the so-called covenant of works (Gen 2:15–17). For Kim, Genesis 1:28 should be interpreted to be a covenant that promises to bless Adam with the kingdom in the context of the Garden of Eden.[8] Kim also argues that the theme of the blessing runs through the entire Scripture, from Genesis to Revelation, and that the blessing God promises to his people is ultimately the eternal kingdom of God, which will be realized and consummated in the new heaven and new earth.[9]

Who Will Enter the Millennial Kingdom?

On the basis of such covenantal hermeneutics, Kim argues that the Lord Jesus Christ will establish the millennial kingdom right after the parousia at the end of the great tribulation. For Kim, the millennial kingdom will be a physical, earthly, and institutional kingdom in the context of this spatio-temporal world. In this sense, Kim views the millennial kingdom as the restoration of Eden. What will the millennial kingdom be like? For Kim, none of the following will be there: Satan (Rev 20:1–3), wars (Isa 2:4;

---

8. Kim, *Go into the Land*, 4–14. I have presented a similar view. See Chung, "Toward the Reformed and Covenantal Theology," 133–46.

9. Kim, *Go into the Land*, 111–44.

Mic 4:3), plagues (Isa 65:23), damage (Isa 65:25), evil people (Isa 14:3–4), or death (Rev 20:4).[10]

Who, then, will enter the millennial kingdom? First of all, the Lord Jesus will be the supreme ruler. Second, those who participate in the first resurrection (Rev 20:6) will rule with Christ. Kim agrees with the traditional historic premillennialist interpretation that *all* the righteous dead, not only the martyrs, will be resurrected at the parousia and that they will enter and rule over the millennial kingdom.

Over whom will these resurrected saints rule with the Lord? Kim argues that it is "the survivors" of the great tribulation who will be ruled over, the ordinary residents of the millennial kingdom. In this context, he appeals to Zechariah 14:16–17: "Then the survivors from all the nations that have attacked Jerusalem will go up year after year to worship the King, the Lord Almighty, and to celebrate the Festival of Tabernacles. If any of the peoples of the earth do not go up to Jerusalem to worship the King, the Lord Almighty, they will have no rain." Who are these survivors? Kim seems to agree with the traditional historic premillennialist interpretation proffered by Ladd and Blomberg—i.e., that it is the unrighteous survivors who will enter the millennial kingdom and continue to reproduce, some of their descendants of whom will become Gog and Magog and will be deceived by Satan to rebel against the Lord at the end of the millennial kingdom.[11]

Kim's view of the new heaven and new earth is consistent with the traditional historic premillennialist interpretation of Revelation 21–22. For Kim, while the millennial kingdom will be established in the context of this spatio-temporal world, the new heaven and new earth will be eternal in nature, which means it will transcend the limitations of time and space. Kim believes that the eternal state is harmonized and consistent with physicality and materiality in a glorified sense. The new heaven and new earth will be the eternal kingdom of God.[12]

10. Kim, *What Will Take Place*, 254.
11. Kim, *What Will Take Place*, 254.
12. Kim, *What Will Take Place*, 255.

The Two Witnesses of Revelation 11

One of the distinctive aspects of Kim's eschatology is his interpretation of the two witnesses of Revelation 11. At the outset, it is important to appreciate that Kim's interpretation of the two witnesses is in line with Byeong Seok Min's and Gwang Bok Lee's interpretations. However, Kim's perspective is different from that of Lee, who has a tendency to limit the commission of the two witnesses to ordained ministers alone.

First of all, Kim argues that the two witnesses are not two literal figures like Moses, Elijah, or John the Baptist, but rather a *group* of servants whom God will raise and commission during the great tribulation. Second, these servants of the last days will be given two kinds of mission: one political and the other religious. Their political mission will be similar to Moses's mission during the exodus. They will have to protect, take care of, and arm the church with the power of the Holy Spirit. By contrast, their religious mission will be analogous to Elijah's mission to prophesy against Ahab. So the two witnesses will prophesy against the Antichrist and be persecuted and martyred. Ultimately, however, they will be resurrected and will ascend into heaven.[13]

Exodus from Egypt and Exodus from Babylon

It is another distinctive of Kim's eschatology that he views the ten plagues of the book of Exodus as prefiguring the types of plagues that the seven trumpets and seven bowls bring about in the last times. In that sense, the book of Revelation is a book about the church's exodus from Babylon, the last empire led and reigned by the Antichrist.

According to Kim, the people of Israel were not raptured or removed from the land of Egypt before the outbreak of the plagues, but rather they remained there. In other words, while God was pouring out the plagues of judgment upon the Egyptians, the Israelites were present in the land of Egypt and yet they were

---

13. Kim, *What Will Take Place*, 250.

protected and preserved completely. Likewise, the church will not be raptured while God pours out the plagues of judgment upon the people and land of eschatological Babylon.[14]

Drawing such analogies between the Israelite exodus from Egypt and the church's eschatological exodus from "Babylon" strengthens Kim's own posttribulational perspective. As a historic premillennialist, Kim believes that the dispensational view of a *pre*tribulational rapture is inconsistent with the teachings of Scripture. Both the exodus from Egypt and the eschatological exodus from "Babylon" occur while God's people remain in the land—upon which the plagues of divine judgment are poured. The people of God suffer tribulation and hardship, while experiencing God's miraculous and faithful protection and preservation.

Byeong Seok Min (b. 1935): Reformed Premillennialism

Byeong Seok Min graduated from Chongshin University of Korea and served as pastor at Shinseng Church for many years. Though not a professionally trained scholar, he supported historic premillennialism as an influential pastor. He also led popular Revelation seminars, beginning in 1987, to teach biblical eschatology to pastors and lay Christians. Not only that, he founded Bamjoongsori Ministry after his formal retirement to educate believers eschatologically, particularly from a historic premillennial perspective.[15] He also published a few dozen books on the topic, the most representative ones including *Reformed Premillennialism, The First Resurrection and the Millennium, Daniel's Eschatological Vision, Studying the Book of Revelation,* and *Revelation of the End Times.* Min thus contributed greatly to the spread of historic premillennialism in Korea.

---

14. Kim, *Revelation Bible Study,* 184–88.

15. See Bamjoongsori Ministry's website (in Korean) at www.bamjoongsori.org.

Eschatological Framework

In order to examine Min's eschatology, I will analyze his magnum opus, *Reformed Premillennialism*. Here, he generally adopts the historic premillennial framework. For example, his hermeneutical approach is more in line with traditional Reformed covenant theology than dispensationalism, not privileging Jews over gentiles. In addition, his view of the rapture is posttribulational, which means that for him the church will go through the great tribulation and will be taken up to welcome the Lord at the parousia.

The First Resurrection

Where Min differs from traditional historic premillennialism is his denial that *all* deceased believers will be resurrected at Jesus's return. According to Min, only *Christian martyrs* will be resurrected at this time. He argues that it is only the resurrected martyrs and the Christians who suffer the great tribulation who will partake in the blessings of the millennial kingdom.

According to his interpretation of Revelation 20:4–5, those who participate in the first resurrection will be composed of two groups. The first group consists of "the souls of those who had been beheaded because of their testimony about Jesus and because of the word of God" (Rev 20:4a). These are martyrs who have been killed before the rise of the Antichrist.[16] The second group consists of those who "had not worshiped the beast or its image and had not received its mark on their foreheads or their hands" (v. 4b). For Min, these are martyrs who have been killed by the Antichrist during the great tribulation.[17] Therefore, according to Min, only these martyrs will participate in the first resurrection and will reign with the Lord Jesus in the millennial kingdom.

Why, then, does Scripture divide the martyrs of the first resurrection into two groups? According to Min, it is because Revelation 6:11 must be fulfilled. "Then each of them was given

16. Min, *Reformed Premillennialism*, 26.
17. Min, *Reformed Premillennialism*, 27.

a white robe, and they were told to wait a little longer, until the full number of their fellow servants, their brothers and sisters, were killed just as they had been." This verse reveals that the martyrs who had already been killed should wait for the full number of their fellow servants to be killed during the great tribulation. For Min, these servants are the two witnesses who will engage in prophetic ministry for 1,260 days, who will fight against the Antichrist, who will be killed and resurrected, and who will ascend into heaven (Rev 11:7–12).[18]

For Min, after the first resurrection of the parousia, the millennial kingdom will follow and then there will be another resurrection at the end of the millennium. Revelation 20:5 states, "(The rest of the dead did not come to life until the thousand years were ended.) This is the first resurrection." Who are the "rest of the dead"? Both the righteous and the unrighteous dead who did not participate in the first resurrection, says Min.

It is evident from the above discussion that Min's interpretation of the first resurrection is considerably different from the traditional Western historic premillennial position, according to which all believers, martyred or not, will be resurrected at the parousia. Of course, there are a few Western exegetes who interpret Revelation 20:4–5 similarly, including Robert H. Mounce[19] and Gordon D. Fee.[20] Nevertheless, it is undeniable that Min's interpretation of these verses is distinct and unique in the Korean context.

On the basis of the above discussion, Min criticizes the traditional historic premillennial interpretation of the first resurrection and the millennial kingdom. He argues that if all of the deceased believers are resurrected and all of the believers alive at the time are transformed simultaneously at the parousia, then their abode must be the eternal New Jerusalem, not the earthly millennium. How can believers with spiritual and resurrected bodies lead an earthly life on earth? Who will reproduce in the millennial kingdom if only the resurrected and transformed believers live in the

18. Min, *Reformed Premillennialism*, 27.
19. Mounce, *Book of Revelation*, 345–78.
20. Fee, *Revelation*, 279–83.

millennium? If they can reproduce, then when will their offspring be resurrected? If their offspring do not die and stay alive until the end of the millennium, then when will they be transformed? Many difficult and complex questions remain unresolved.[21] Min's questions seem to be valid and legitimate.

Of course, according to traditional historic premillennialism, unbelievers who are still alive at the parousia will enter the millennial kingdom, along with the resurrected and transformed believers, and they will reproduce. And some of them will rebel against God following the deception of Satan, who is released at the end of the millennium. From Min's perspective, the traditional interpretations remain unsatisfactory.

In support of his own interpretation of the first resurrection, Min appeals to 1 Corinthians 15:22–26:

> For as in Adam all die, so in Christ all will be made alive. But each in turn: Christ, the firstfruits; then, when he comes, those who belong to him. Then the end will come, when he hands over the kingdom to God the Father after he has destroyed all dominion, authority and power. For he must reign until he has put all his enemies under his feet. The last enemy to be destroyed is death.

For Min, this passage talks about the order of the resurrection of Christians, not of unbelievers. After the resurrection of Jesus Christ, the firstfruits, there will be the resurrection of "those who belong to him when he comes" (v. 23). This means that at the parousia "those who belong to him" will be resurrected. And after their resurrection, there will be another resurrection when the end comes—that is, when Jesus "hands over the kingdom to God the Father after he has destroyed all dominion, authority and power" (v. 24). When will this occur—at the parousia or at the great white throne? On the basis of the correlation between v. 26 and Revelation 20:14, Min believes this to occur at the great white throne. Therefore, Min argues that there will be two resurrections of Christians, the first at the parousia and the next at the very end of human history—that

---

21. Min, *Reformed Premillennialism*, 31–32.

is, at the judgment of the great white throne.[22] In this light, Min interprets 1 Corinthians 15:22–23 as meaning that there is an order in the resurrection of Christians.

Who, then, are "those who belong to Christ," those who will be resurrected at the parousia? Are they all the believers or only the martyrs? Answering these questions, Min appeals to Revelation 17:14, "They will wage war against the Lamb, but the Lamb will triumph over them because he is Lord of lords and King of kings—and with him will be his called, chosen and faithful followers." He identifies "those who belong to him" in 1 Corinthians 15:23 with "his called, chosen, and faithful followers" in Revelation 17:14. For Min, these are the martyrs to which Revelation 20:4–5 refers. Furthermore, he identifies these people with "the armies of heaven" in Revelation 19:14, whereas traditional historic premillennialists interpret "the armies of heaven" as angels or, alternatively, all the resurrected and transformed believers.[23]

The Transformation of Believers

On the basis of his argument for the first resurrection, in which only martyrs will participate at the parousia, Min contends that the transformation of believers will occur not at the parousia but at the end of the millennium. Thus, Min rejects the traditional historic premillennialist interpretation of 1 Thessalonians 4:13–18.

> Brothers and sisters, we do not want you to be uninformed about those who sleep in death, so that you do not grieve like the rest of mankind, who have no hope. For we believe that Jesus died and rose again, and so we believe that God will bring with Jesus those who have fallen asleep in him. According to the Lord's word, we tell you that we who are still alive, who are left until the coming of the Lord, will certainly not precede those who have fallen asleep. For the Lord himself will come down from heaven, with a loud command, with the voice of

---

22. Min, *Reformed Premillennialism*, 33.
23. Min, *Reformed Premillennialism*, 35–36.

the archangel and with the trumpet call of God, and the dead in Christ will rise first. After that, we who are still alive and are left will be caught up together with them in the clouds to meet the Lord in the air. And so we will be with the Lord forever. Therefore encourage one another with these words.

According to the traditional interpretation, this passage refers to the parousia and the rapture of believers, as well as the transformation of believers into their resurrected bodies, which will occur when they are raptured at the parousia. In other words, the traditional historic premillennial interpretation connects closely 1 Thessalonians 4:13–18 with 1 Corinthians 15:51–52, which states, "Listen, I tell you a mystery: We will not all sleep, but we will all be changed—in a flash, in the twinkling of an eye, at the last trumpet. For the trumpet will sound, the dead will be raised imperishable, and we will be changed."

In stark contrast, Min argues that the transformation of believers into their resurrected bodies will not occur at the parousia but at the end of the millennium, before the great white throne. Therefore, according to Min, at the judgment of the great white throne two groups of people, both the righteous dead and the unrighteous dead, will be resurrected. And those believers who live throughout the millennium will be transformed into their resurrected bodies.

In relation to Min's unique interpretation of 1 Thessalonians 4:13–18, a valid question should be raised. When v. 16 says that "the dead in Christ will rise first," does the verse not mean that all the dead in Christ will rise, not merely the martyrs? In response, Min contends that this verse provides only a partial revelation about the resurrection of believers, not a total revelation. First Corinthians 15:22–26, by contrast, provides a total revelation. So, for Min, 1 Thessalonians 4:16 must be interpreted in light of 1 Corinthians 15:22–26.[24]

---

24. Min, *Reformed Premillennialism*, 51.

People and Life in the Millennium

Who will enter the millennial kingdom? Min argues that the Lord Jesus Christ will reign with the resurrected martyrs who participate in the first resurrection. In addition, the believers who remain alive at the parousia will enter the millennium and will be subject to the rule of Christ and these resurrected martyrs.[25] When they enter the millennium, they will still have their natural, not transformed or resurrected, bodies. Therefore, these believers will be able to reproduce.

What will the millennium be like? Min argues that since Satan will be bound completely for a thousand years, the residents of the millennium will not be tempted or deceived until he is released at the end of the millennium. According to Min, the millennium will be free from the curse of sin and the residents of the millennium will not experience death. Although the believers, the residents of the millennium, will still have a sin nature, they will not commit sins because Satan will not be able to tempt and deceive them and because the millennium will be filled with the righteousness of God.[26] Min argues, "Sin cannot exist in the world where Christ reigns with righteousness. In a new Eden filled with God's justice there will be no presence of sin against God's justice."[27] Therefore, according to Min, the millennium will be a restoration of pre-fall Eden in the context of this spatio-temporal universe, not of the eternal new heaven and new earth.

Min argues that Old Testament prophecies about the messianic kingdom will be fulfilled in the millennium. Foremost among these is Isaiah 65:17–25, a prophecy about the millennium:

> "See, I will create new heavens and a new earth. The former things will not be remembered, nor will they come to mind. But be glad and rejoice forever in what I will create, for I will create Jerusalem to be a delight and its people a joy. I will rejoice over Jerusalem and

---

25. Min, *Reformed Premillennialism*, 125.
26. Min, *Reformed Premillennialism*, 127.
27. Min, *Reformed Premillennialism*, 127.

take delight in my people; the sound of weeping and of crying will be heard in it no more. Never again will there be in it an infant who lives but a few days, or an old man who does not live out his years; the one who dies at a hundred will be thought a mere child; the one who fails to reach a hundred will be considered accursed. They will build houses and dwell in them; they will plant vineyards and eat their fruit. No longer will they build houses and others live in them, or plant and others eat. For as the days of a tree, so will be the days of my people; my chosen ones will long enjoy the work of their hands. They will not labor in vain, nor will they bear children doomed to misfortune; for they will be a people blessed by the LORD, they and their descendants with them. Before they call I will answer; while they are still speaking I will hear. The wolf and the lamb will feed together, and the lion will eat straw like the ox, and dust will be the serpent's food. They will neither harm nor destroy on all my holy mountain," says the LORD.

Min believes that these prophecies about the millennium will be fulfilled almost literally. They are neither symbolic nor parabolic expressions about the age of the gospel. Rather, these are about blessings believers will enjoy in the millennial kingdom after the Lord's second coming.[28]

The 144,000 Servants and the Two Witnesses

Min presents a very intriguing interpretation of the 144,000 servants in Revelation 7 and 14. He argues that the number 144,000 does not symbolize the witnessing church or the faithful remnants of the church in the last days or throughout the church age, as some Western historic premillennialists have interpreted it. For example, Mounce has argued, "It seems more likely . . . that they are not two individuals but a symbol of the witnessing church in the last tumultuous days before the end of the age."[29] In a similar

---

28. Min, *Reformed Premillennialism*, 128–29.
29. Mounce, *Book of Revelation*, 217.

vein, some scholars in this group have identified the two witnesses of Revelation 11 with a large group of witnesses. For example, dispensationalist Arno C. Gaebelein has argued: "Perhaps the leaders would be two great instruments, manifesting the spirit of Moses and Elijah, endowed with supernatural power, but a larger number of witnesses is unquestionably in view here."[30] According to Steve Gregg, Ladd, the most well-known historic premillennialist of the past century, takes a similar approach. Gregg states:

> Ladd takes this approach as well, allowing that "Possibly there is a blending of the symbolic and the specific" in the passage. He believes the witnesses to be two "actual historical eschatological personages who will be sent to Israel to bring about her conversion." He elaborates that the two witnesses may indeed represent the witness of the church to Israel throughout the age.[31]

Gregg's summary implies that Ladd was open to the interpretation that identifies the two witnesses of Revelation 11 as a large number of the witnesses throughout the history of the church. William Hendriksen, an amillennialist, takes a similar approach. He argues that "[t]hese witnesses symbolize the Church militant bearing testimony through its ministers and missionaries throughout the present dispensations."[32] Blomberg's conclusion is similar as well. He argues that "whether the entire church or just Jewish Christians (or post-rapture Christians) live through the tribulation, it is natural to view these two witnesses as symbolic or representative of all God's faithful, witnessing followers during this awful period at the end of human history as we know it."[33] However, as a historic premillennialist, Blomberg wants to confine the ministry of the two witnesses to the period of tribulation in the last days of human history, arguing that "the two witnesses portray the church of

---

30. Gaebelein, *Revelation*, 70.
31. Gregg, *Revelation*, 231.
32. Hendriksen, *More than Conquerors*, 155.
33. Blomberg, *From Pentecost to Patmos*, 534.

Jesus Christ boldly testifying to the gospel through the power of the Spirit in these last days."[34]

In contrast, Min argues that the 144,000 servants sealed by God are those who will receive special mission from God in the last days. Their mission is to prophesy against the Antichrist by preaching the eternal gospel of the Lord's second coming during the second half of the great tribulation for 1,260 days. Moreover, Min identifies the 144,000 with the two witnesses in Revelation 11. Thus, for Min, the two witnesses are not literally two persons or two prophets, as Charles C. Ryrie and John Walvoord interpreted them. Ryrie summarizes his position as follows:

> This much is certain: (1) They are persons, for all the other times that the word "witness" is used in the New Testament it is used of persons. They are not movements or powers, but individual persons. (2) It is also certain that they are not named in the text, and this writer feels that the case should be left there. These are two exceptional witnesses raised up by God during the Tribulation and preserved by Him until their ministry is completed.[35]

In a similar vein, Walvoord writes: "It seems far preferable to regard these two witnesses as two prophets who will be raised up from among those who turn to Christ in the time of following the rapture."[36]

For Min, the two witnesses are the 144,000 servants who will fulfill their special mission. They will be killed by the Antichrist (11:7) but resurrected after three-and-a-half days (v. 11) and then raptured. They will come together with the Lord as the armies of heaven (19:14) at the parousia. Furthermore, they belong to those who will participate in the first resurrection (20:4). Min's interpretation of the 144,000 servants and the two witnesses is similar to Gwang Bok Lee's. One conspicuous difference between them is that Min does not identify these two witnesses with ordained pastors or ministers. Rather, he seems to argue that both ordained

---

34. Blomberg, *From Pentecost to Patmos*, 536.
35. Ryrie, *Revelation*, 74.
36. Walvoord, *Revelation of Jesus Christ*, 179.

pastors and lay people can receive special mission from God and thus belong to the 144,000 servants.[37]

Gwang Bok Lee (b. 1946): Integrative Historic Premillennialism

Gwang Bok Lee graduated from Chongshin University of Korea and finished the ThM and DRE at Faith Theological Seminary in the United States. He has served as Senior Pastor of Mokyang Church, Adjunct Professor of Practical Theology at Kwangshin University, and Director of the Hindol Mission Center in Korea. He has recently stepped down from Mokyang Church. For the past thirty years, Lee has studied the book of Revelation and the doctrine of eschatology and has authored a number of related books. His magnum opus, *The Complete Collection of Revelation and Biblical Eschatology*, presents in-depth commentary and exegesis of Revelation that clearly resonates with the historic premillennial view. He also adheres closely to a futurist approach to the book.

Throughout the course of his work, Lee has perceived several interpretive weaknesses within historic premillennialism as it developed in the Western theological tradition. Convinced that Scripture lends itself to an eschatology of even greater accuracy, Lee poured his energy into resolving the interpretive dilemmas of the historic premillennial view. According to Lee, there are seven issues that need reform: (1) the presence of the unsaved in the millennium; (2) the problem of Gog and Magog; (3) the hermeneutical link between the millennium in Revelation 20 and the new heavens and new earth in chapter 21; (4) the question of the end-time signs; (5) the seven churches in Revelation 2 and 3; (6) historic premillennialism's quasi-amillennial interpretations; and (7) the proper understanding of other eschatological views. Though a historic premillennialist, Lee studied other eschatological views with consistent effort to accept and incorporate whatever biblically sound and edifying proposition they presented. As a result of this approach, he actively

---

37. Min, *Reformed Premillennialism*, 55–76.

endorses dispensational interpretations of the signs of the second coming and the amillennial emphasis on the spiritual significance of the message of Revelation. Consequently, Lee has formulated a revised version of premillennial eschatology, which he calls "integrative historic premillennialism." It is clear that Lee inherited and spread the historic premillennial view first introduced to Korea by Hyung Ryong Park. It is also observable that Lee's integrative historic premillennialism is an innovative view that uniquely originates within the Asian theological context.

Eschatological Framework

In order to examine Lee's eschatology, I will analyze his *Complete Collection of Revelation and Biblical Eschatology*. Here, he adopts the broad historic premillennial framework. For instance, his hermeneutical approach is more in line with traditional covenant theology than with dispensationalism, not privileging the Jews over the gentiles. And he basically adopts the traditional evangelical methodology of biblical exegesis, which is characterized by grammatical and historical analysis. In addition, his view of the rapture is posttribulational, which means that for him the church will undergo the great tribulation and will be taken up into the sky in order to welcome the Lord at the parousia.

Resurrection and Transformation

Lee agrees with the traditional premillennialist understanding of the resurrection of believers. He argues that all of the righteous dead will rise again at the parousia. Disagreeing with Min, Lee believes that Revelation 20:4–6 does not teach that only the martyrs will be resurrected and reign with Christ in the millennium. Rather, he argues that all believers without exception will be resurrected, and those believers who are alive at the parousia will be transformed. These resurrected and transformed believers will reign with the Lord Jesus Christ in the millennial kingdom.

Furthermore, Lee believes that only the unrighteous dead will be resurrected following the millennial kingdom at the great white throne. Therefore, we can conclude that Lee basically accepts the traditional historic premillennial view of the resurrection and transformation of believers.

Who Will Enter the Millennium?

Although he agrees with the traditional historic premillennial interpretation of the rapture, resurrection, and transformation of believers, his argument about those who enter the millennial kingdom is considerably different from other traditional historic premillennialists.

First of all, Lee argues that all unbelievers will be judged and destroyed completely at the parousia. In other words, no unbelievers will survive the judgment of Christ when the Lord returns. In support, Lee appeals to Revelation 19:15, which states: "Coming out of his mouth is a sharp sword with which to strike down the nations. 'He will rule them with an iron scepter.' He treads the winepress of the fury of the wrath of God Almighty." Lee interprets the word *nations* here as the whole human race rebellious against God. So he believes that all unbelievers will be killed by Christ's sword.[38] Accordingly, Lee argues that only the resurrected and transformed believers will enter the millennial kingdom.[39] Undoubtedly, this interpretation is squarely opposed to the traditional historic premillennial view that surviving unbelievers will enter the millennium.

Who, then, will produce offspring—the very descendants who become Gog and Magog (Rev 20:8)? Interestingly, Lee argues that it is the resurrected and transformed believers who will produce such offspring. For Lee, Isaiah 65:23 prophesies that the residents of the millennium will continue to reproduce. Moreover, Lee contends that God's commission to Adam in Genesis 1:28—i.e.,

38. Lee, *Biblical Eschatology*, 392–93.
39. Lee, *Biblical Eschatology*, 395.

to "be fruitful and increase in number; fill the earth and subdue it and rule over the fish in the sea and the birds in the sky and over every living creature that moves on the ground"—should be fulfilled in the millennium.

The difficulty of this interpretation, however, is whether resurrected humans will be able to reproduce. In Matthew 22:30, the Lord Jesus says, "At the resurrection people will neither marry nor be given in marriage; they will be like the angels in heaven." In saying this, Jesus seems to have meant that there will be no reproduction in the resurrection. In other words, resurrected humans will not be able to give birth because they will be like angels who are, evidently, nonreproductive. But Lee rejects this interpretation, arguing instead that this verse means that there will be no marriage in the resurrection (not that there will be no reproduction).[40] He also claims that resurrected believers will reproduce although we do not know the method of reproduction.

Revelation 21–22: The Millennium or the Eternal New Heaven and New Earth?

Another of Lee's somewhat idiosyncratic interpretations of Revelation is that for him chapters 21–22 are about the millennial kingdom, not the eternal state of the new heaven and new earth. Accordingly, chapter 20 is a general introduction to the millennial kingdom and chapters 21–22 are about the blessings of that kingdom. In the Western context, one is hard pressed to find a single exegete or theologian who interprets these chapters in this way.

What, then, are the evidences for Lee's interpretation? First, Jesus Christ came to restore the Garden of Eden, which was lost because of the rebellion of the first parents. So, for Lee, it is natural for the Bible to end its redemptive story with the restoration of the earthly paradise, that is, the millennial kingdom on earth, not eternal heaven.[41] Second, Revelation 21:2 states that the New Jerusalem

---

40. Lee, *Biblical Eschatology*, 398.
41. Lee, *Biblical Eschatology*, 400–401.

came down out of heaven from God. For Lee, this means that the raptured believers came down from the sky after welcoming the Lord at the parousia. So the new heaven and new earth in Revelation 21-22 must be the millennial kingdom on earth.[42] Third, 2 Peter 3:13 talks about "a new heaven and a new earth" and connects it with the parousia rather than the great white throne. Thus, the new heaven and new earth in Revelation 21-22 should be the millennial kingdom, not eternal heaven.[43] Fourth, Isaiah 65:17-25 also describes a new heaven and a new earth, connecting it with the millennial kingdom rather than an eternal state. Thus, Revelation 21-22 should be interpreted to depict the millennial kingdom rather than an eternal state.[44] Fifth, Lee argues that although the millennial kingdom can be described in comparison with the current world, the eternal state cannot be depicted since it is the world of God. How can human language with definite limitations describe the eternal state, which is the perfect world of God?[45] The answer is that it cannot. Therefore, Lee argues that the new heaven and new earth in Revelation 21-22 must be viewed as a description of blessings available in the earthy millennial kingdom.

The Two Witnesses of Revelation 11

Lee presents a very distinct interpretation of the two witnesses of Revelation 11, which is similar to Min's. First of all, for Lee, these two witnesses are not two literal individuals—whether a literal Moses and Elijah or Enoch and Elijah—but rather a large number of people whom God will raise for special purposes at the end of human history, probably during the great tribulation and right before the rise of the Antichrist. For Lee, God's servants for final harvest will be ordained ministers of the Word of God or pastors of local churches rather than ordinary lay Christians. In other words, he

---

42. Lee, *Biblical Eschatology*, 402.
43. Lee, *Biblical Eschatology*, 402.
44. Lee, *Biblical Eschatology*, 402.
45. Lee, *Biblical Eschatology*, 402-3.

confines the qualifications of these two witnesses to ordained pastors. In his interpretation of the book more generally, Lee seems to distinguish rather sharply ordained ministers from ordinary lay believers. Second, the two witnesses of Revelation 11 will be commissioned to prepare the way for the Lord's return by prophesying about his imminent coming, convicting people of their sins, and urging them to repent. Third, the two witnesses will receive supernatural and miraculous power from God and will exercise their power until they finish their task of prophesying against the world. Fourth, they will be killed by the Antichrist but resurrected by the power of God. Fifth, and closely related, they will follow the examples of Moses, Elijah, John the Baptist, and Jesus Christ, whose pattern of life is characterized by bearing the cross of contempt, disgrace, persecution, suffering, tribulation, and even death. Sixth, the two witnesses will finally experience the ultimate victory over the power of evil by being resurrected and vindicated by the power of Jesus Christ. Seventh, they are identifiable as the "144,000 servants of God" in Revelation 7 and 14.[46]

Critical Engagement

Hyung Ryong Park's historic premillennialism seems very similar to the traditional historic premillennialism advocated by Ladd and others in the Western context. In particular, in terms of the question of who will enter the millennial kingdom and reproduce, Park argues that unbelievers who survive the great tribulation will enter the millennial kingdom and will give birth to their descendants. Moreover, some of their descendants, whom Revelation 20 calls Gog and Magog, will be deceived by Satan and rebel against God. In addition, in terms of the resurrection of human beings, he attributes the first resurrection of Revelation 20:4 to all of the righteous dead, arguing that following the millennial kingdom all the unrighteous dead will be raised to face judgment at the great white throne.

---

46. Lee, *Biblical Eschatology*, 579–613.

Like Park's premillennial views, Hyung Tae Kim's historic premillennialism also seems consistent with traditional historic premillennialism in the West. One of the distinctive points of his eschatology is that he combines traditional Reformed covenantal theology and kingdom hermeneutics, presenting a creative and persuasive framework for eschatological discussions. In particular, he goes beyond the threefold covenantal scheme of traditional Reformed theology by interpreting Genesis 1:28 as a covenant of kingdom prior to the covenant of works in Genesis 2:16–17. This is a very meaningful advancement in terms of biblical and eschatological hermeneutics.

In addition, by means of typological hermeneutics Kim interprets the ten plagues of the book of Exodus as a prefiguring shadow of the plagues (i.e., the seven seals, seven trumpets, and seven bowls) of the last exodus from "Babylon," arguing that just as the Israelites were miraculously protected from those plagues, so the church will be protected from the eschatological plagues. This entails that the church will not be raptured but rather that it will remain on earth and undergo the great tribulation. Thus, for Kim, the notion of a posttribulational rapture is the only valid and veracious option. Furthermore, Kim's interpretation of the identity of the two witnesses of Revelation 11 seems legitimate, especially in view of similar interpretations of Byeong Seok Min and Gwang Bok Lee.

Byeong Seok Min's "reformed premillennialism" has many commendable features. In particular, Min's analysis of the order of the resurrections of the righteous dead seems persuasive. In light of the logical flow of 1 Corinthians 15:22–24, which seems to teach the order of the resurrections of those in Christ, Min's argument warrants further exploration. Furthermore, his notion of the millennial kingdom as the restoration of the Garden of Eden appears convincing. In addition, his proposal about those who will enter the millennial kingdom is fascinating. For Min, only the resurrected martyrs and surviving believers will enter the millennium, and it is these believers who will continue to reproduce, giving birth to descendants who will be deceived by Satan and who will rebel against God at the end of the millennial kingdom. More than anything else, Min's interpretation of the 144,000 servants and the two witnesses as those specially commissioned during the second half of the great tribulation is intriguing and convincing.

However, his exegesis of 1 Thessalonians 4:13–18 is questionable because v. 16 of this passage seems to imply that all of the righteous dead will be resurrected at the parousia, as the traditional premillennial interpretation would have it. Moreover, Min's exegeses of other passages such as 1 Corinthians 15:20–26 are questionable on the basis of a more rigorous analysis of the original text. Nevertheless, it is undeniable that Min's proposal is refreshing and deserves scholarly attention.

In a similar vein, Gwang Bok Lee has also presented an alternative to traditional historic premillennialism, naming his position "integrative historic premillennialism." Lee's proposals are innovative and have a certain element of truth. However, they are also highly questionable. In particular, his notion that only resurrected and transformed believers will enter the millennial kingdom and that it is these believers who will continue to reproduce seems to be inconsistent with Matthew 22:30.

Furthermore, Lee's interpretation of Revelation 21–22 as a depiction of the blessings of the millennial kingdom rather than of the eternal state of the new heavens and new earth is intriguing and somewhat persuasive, but it is still questionable. This is especially true because his view of eternity appears Platonic and dualistic: he seems to deny materiality and physicality to eternity. However, it is very important to appreciate that the universe will maintain its physical and material character even in its eternal state. Scripture repeatedly emphasizes that eternity is absolutely compatible with physicality and materiality. Of course, one can glean some important insights from Lee's argument here. Nevertheless, a better understanding of Revelation 21–22 is that it depicts the eternal state of the new heavens and new earth.

Finally, most of Lee's arguments for the identity of the two witnesses are persuasive and consistent with biblical principles. However, the biblical text does not support his sharp distinction between ordained ministers and non-ordained lay Christians. Rather, Revelation 11 seems to assume that all Christians who will remain faithful to their Lord and Savior can become God's servants for final harvest.

Conclusion

Over the course of the past century, Asian theologians, especially Korean theologians, have been endeavoring to advance historic premillennialism in accordance with the teachings of Scripture. As a result, theologians such as Hyung Tae Kim, Byeong Seok Min, and Gwang Bok Lee have presented alternative interpretations of important eschatological themes, including the resurrections of the righteous and unrighteous dead, the residents of the millennial kingdom, the two witnesses of Revelation 11, and the 144,000 servants of chapters 7 and 14. After introducing their perspectives, we have critically evaluated their innovative proposals.

Despite these critical reflections, we should appreciate that these Asian theologians have attempted to be faithful to the teachings of Scripture. Their endeavors should be appreciated and commended. However, we should test their proposals against Scripture, accepting what is insightful and setting aside what is erroneous. Ultimately, this is what we should do in order to remain faithful to the eschatological teachings of Scripture.

Concluding Reflections on Premillennialism

THE PURPOSE OF THIS chapter is to make some concluding reflections on the previous essays on the variety of premillennial positions. More specifically, we will focus on the primary issues hermeneutically and theologically that influence the way the interpreter understands the meaning and purpose of the millennium from Revelation 20, by way of comparison and contrast. Obviously, much will have to do with the interpretive and theological presuppositions that the readers brings to the task of interpreting the relevant biblical texts and how one decides to put the biblical data together within a larger framework. Yet all sides agree that the biblical texts themselves, however understood, must play the determinate role in our understanding of the millennium. The following discussion is not exhaustive, but focuses on only a handful of the major issues at play in the interpretation of the millennium.

The Context of the Millennium

When considering context, the interpreter thinks naturally of the immediate literary context of a given biblical text. However, context can extend much broader to eventually include the entire canonical, biblical-theological context. A key factor in interpreting the millennium, especially from Revelation 20:1–6, has to do with the context that one privileges in understanding the thousand years from Revelation 20. One approach is to focus exclusively on the book of Revelation itself as the dominant context, and ask what role the millennium plays in the book itself, and especially in the concluding visions in chapters 19–22. Those who focus primarily, if not exclusively, on the context of Revelation itself note the lack of specific details in Revelation 20:1–6 as to where the millennium takes place and what happens there. There is no clear reference to whether the millennium transpires on earth or in heaven. And John says nothing about what happens there, over whom the saints rule, conditions in the millennium, who populates the millennium, whether there will be reproduction, and the like. Furthermore, this approach would draw attention to the fact that Revelation 20:1–6 is the only place in the entire Bible that unequivocally teaches a thousand-year reign (though this does not mean that it would be entirely novel or inconsistent with other OT and NT texts). They would also note that the millennium, in the context of Satan's previous mistreatment of the Saints, as well as his final judgment here, functions primarily to vindicate the saints and indicate their victory. In this life Satan put them to death and reigned over them, now the saints come to life and they reign. Thus, in its context the sole function of Revelation is to depict the judgment of evil, the final vindication of the saints and their ultimate triumph. We labelled this view the thematic millennial view.

However, the interpreter can choose to expand the context and give priority to the broader biblical theological context, particularly the OT development of the theme of kingdom of God and its fulfillment in the NT. In particular, both classic and progressive dispensational approaches to the millennium, and to a large extent historical premillennial views (including those in an Asian context), would read it in light of OT promises of the establishment of God's kingdom on earth, where his Messiah will reign over the earth and all the nations (e.g., Isaiah 65; Ezekiel 36–37). That is, the millennium in Revelation 20:1–6 is the fulfillment of the messianic age prophesied in the OT in which God's kingdom will be established on earth and his Messiah will rule. The silence about what takes place in the millennium and its meaning in Revelation 20:1-6 is broken when one turns to the OT, and reads the millennium *in light of* the broader redemptive-historical context and movement in the OT and NT. Even then, how they understand the relationship between the OT texts and their fulfillment in the millennium differs. For classic dispensationalists the millennium appears to be more of a finale, the climax of God's promises to his people, especially Israel, on this earth. This will then be followed by the eternal state. For both progressive dispensationalists and historical premillennialists the millennium is only a further stage (though an important one) in the progressive outworking of God's redemptive purposes to establish his kingdom on earth, the ultimate fulfillment, with varying degrees of discontinuity with the present creation, coming in the new creation (Rev 21:1—22:5). For historical premillennialists, Israel does not play the key role that it does in more dispensational approaches to the millennium. Furthermore, for some historical premillennial approaches, especially those produced in an Asian context, there is often detailed description of life in the millennium: e.g., Jerusalem will be rebuilt, the nation of Israel will be converted, peace and righteousness will prevail, there will be fruitfulness and abundance, and there will be a return to Eden-like conditions (see Genesis 1-3).

Literal vs. Symbolic Interpretation

At first glance an important issue would seem to be how literally or symbolically one interprets the reference to the millennium from Revelation 20:1-6. Obviously, if one interprets the millennium literally (an actual period lasting a thousand calendar years) then it will refer to a specific period of a thousand years in duration in between the final battle in 19:11-21 and the establishment of the new creation in 21:1—22:5. Classical dispensationalists tend to interpret this as a literal period of time, coupled with a specific view of the fulfillment of OT prophesy, so that the millennium becomes the place where Israel's promises are fulfilled. But a symbolic approach that sees the millennium symbolizing a period of time that is not necessarily a literal thousand years in duration could still see the millennium as a literal period of time that functions as a transition between this present age and the establishment of the final form of the kingdom in the new creation. Historical premillennialists, and some progressive dispensationalists, would treat the millennium in this manner. Thus, they would take seriously the millennium as an actual period of time of some duration that serves as a transitional stage of the kingdom between this age and the new creation, but it is referred to with the *symbol* of a thousand years. The main difference, then, is not so much to be framed in terms of literal vs. symbolic interpretation, but how one fits the pieces of the OT and NT puzzle together more generally, as well as other theological and hermeneutical commitments one brings to the task of interpreting the millennium. With their view of the relationship of the OT to the NT and understanding of fulfillment, and the sharp distinction between Israel and the church, classic dispensationalists will tend to see the millennium more of an end all due to its very specific purpose of bringing to fulfillment the OT prophecies of the promises that are to be given to Israel (e.g., land, temple). They must be fulfilled to Israel in their land on this earth. With progressive dispensationalists, and even more so for historical premillennialists, their understanding of the progressive outworking and fulfillment of the promises of God at the first coming of Christ, then in the church, and at the future coming of Christ, means that the millennium does not play as distinctive of a role, but again functions as one stage (albeit a greater one and an important one) in the progressive outworking of God's plan to establish his kingdom on earth, which climaxes with the new creation. Like its classical cousin, progressive dispensationalism would still see an important role for Israel in the outworking of God's promises on earth, but not to the exclusion of the gentiles or the importance of the new creation as the climax of God's *earthly* (see the next section) redemptive purposes. Likewise, some Asian approaches to the millennium would interpret it rather literally, with a rebuilt Jerusalem, abundance, and fruitfulness, including a role for converted Israel.

CONCLUDING REFLECTIONS ON PREMILLENNIALISM

Still, a symbolic interpretation of the millennium does open up a broader range of options for understanding the millennium. Thus, the thematic millennial view sees the one thousand years as a symbol of the vindication of the saints at the second coming of Christ, but does not refer to a specific period of time at all, at least not of any duration (obviously Christ's coming takes place in time).[1] The thousand years contributes the meaning of completeness and magnitude, and is not meant to communicate a temporal piece of information. More important is what the temporal designation is meant to symbolize, or what meanings and thematics are being communicated.

Who Populates the Millennium?

One important issue raised by premillennial approaches to Revelation 20:4–6 is who populates the millennial kingdom on earth. Who will enter the millennial kingdom? That is, where do the people come from, many of which Satan is able to deceive for a final, last-ditch effort to defeat the people of God in vv. 7–10? That is, there appears to be both believers and non-believers present during the millennium. This question is avoided altogether by a thematic approach to the millennium, which does not see the millennium as a specific period of time at all, and which does not see Revelation 20:4–6 specifying where the millennium takes place (heaven or earth?). The point is the theological themes communicated by the image of the millennium, not a detailed picture of what takes place there. This view would see other premillennial approaches as creating unnecessary complications.

The typical historical premillennial response to this issue is to see all Christians as being resurrected in 20:4–6, and then

---

1. This is in contrast to those progressive dispensationalists and historical premillennialists who take the reference to the thousand as symbolic, but still referring to a period of time of some duration. It is also in contrast to the (non-premillennial) view known as *amillennialism*, which sees the thousand YEARS as symbolic of a period of time that extends from the first coming of Christ to his second coming.

unbelievers who survive the tribulation and judgment (chap. 19) as entering the millennium and populating the earth at this time. These are the ones that Satan is able to deceive in a final assault on the people of God (20:7–10). This creates the issue of having resurrected and natural bodies in the millennium at the same time, an issue that may be alleviated by noting that the resurrected Jesus in the Gospels interacted with his followers while they were still in their natural bodies. One significant deviation to this view is that of Gwang Bok Lee, who sees only resurrected, transformed believers as entering the millennium. According to him they are actually able to reproduce and populate the millennium. In any case, those that understand the millennium as a period of time of some length between the second coming of Christ and the new creation/eternal state must account for those that appear in vv. 7–10 at the end of the millennium after the judgment of 19:11–21 has taken place.

The Relationship to the New Creation (Revelation 21:1—22:5)

Another important issue that impinges on one's understanding of the millennium is the role that the new creation (Rev 21:1—22:5) plays in our interpretation, and its relationship to the millennium. To put the question more specifically, what is the extent of *continuity* or *discontinuity* between this present creation and the new creation? The more discontinuity one sees between the two, the more necessary it becomes to find God's promises of his rule and blessings on earth fulfilled in a millennium on this present earth. In this case, the millennium becomes theologically necessary as a period of time on this *earth*, since God's promises and purposes for earth must be vindicated on this earth, not in some eternal state. This is true to varying degrees for the classic dispensational, progressive dispensational, and historical premillennial views. Classic dispensational approaches to the millennium have tended to see more discontinuity between this earth and the eternal state; the millennium is where God's promises to Israel will be ultimately fulfilled, involving restoration to the land, the theocratic rule of David's Son, etc. For progressive dispensational and historical premillennial views there is both continuity and discontinuity between this present earth and the new creation. However, there is still an emphasis on the need for God's promises and purposes to be fulfilled on this present earth. Within an Asian context, Hyung Tae Kim concludes that the new heavens and new earth transcend time and space. Gwang Bok Lee's approach within a historical premillennial understanding is somewhat unique, even within an Asian context, in that he interprets Revelation 21-22 as a description of the earthly millennium. According to him, the eternal state after the millennium is so qualitatively different from this world that it cannot be described in human language. Thus, the rather physical description found in 21:1—22:5 must be of the millennium in 20:4-6, not the eternal state. For Lee there is strong (if not complete) discontinuity between the millennium on this earth and the eternal state.

The thematic millennial view sees both continuity and discontinuity, but would emphasize more the continuity between this earth and the new creation, the discontinuity pointing to the transformation and renewal of this earth that takes place in the new creation. That is, the new *earth* in Revelation 21:1 is *this earth*, but renewed, redeemed, transformed, and restored, much in the same way that our resurrection bodies will be our bodies redeemed and transformed (there will both continuity and discontinuity between our present bodies and our resurrection bodies; but they will be our bodies nevertheless). In this way the millennium is not needed in order for the *earthly* promises of the OT to find their fulfillment. The new creation performs this task nicely.

Conclusion

There are numerous factors that feed into one's approach to the millennium and the interpretation of Revelation 20:4-6. For this reason, interpretation of the millennium is fraught with complexities, so that many despair of arriving at any kind of settled interpretation. This is true not only among the different major millennial positions (amillennial, postmillennial, premillennial), but as this book has demonstrated within premillennialism itself. Yet we are convinced that the interpreter cannot throw up his/her hands in despair and ignore this important issue and text. Since we are dealing with God's very revelation to his people, such an approach is not an option, no matter how difficult and involved the task. But the main purpose of this book has not been to provide instruction on how to arrive at a millennial position, but only to demonstrate the diversity of views within premillennialism and to point out some of the issues, hermeneutically and theologically, in arriving at a solution. I have only surveyed some of the larger contextual and theological issues that must be weighed and integrated into any millennial perspective. Yet at the end of the day one must ultimately justify one's position though exegesis of the biblical texts themselves, especially Revelation 20:4–6. If the interpreter comes away with a greater appreciation for the variations of positions within just one millennial movement (premillennialism) and is driven back to a careful examination of the text of Scripture, this book will have served its purpose.

Bibliography

Allison, Gregg R. *Historical Theology: An Introduction to Christian Doctrine*. Grand Rapids: Zondervan, 2011.
Bateman, Herbert W. *Three Central Issues in Contemporary Dispensationalism: A Comparison of Traditional and Progressive Views*. Grand Rapids: Kregel, 1999.
Bauckham, R. J. *The Climax of Prophecy: Studies on the Book of Revelation*. Edinburgh: T. & T. Clark, 1993.
———. *Theology of the Book of Revelation*. Cambridge: Cambridge University Press, 1993.
Beasley-Murray, George R. *The Book of Revelation*. London: Marshall, Morgan & Scott, 1978.
———. *Jesus and the Last Days: The Interpretation of the Olivet Discourse*. 1993. Reprint. Vancouver, BC: Regent College, 2005.
Blackstone, William E. *Jesus Is Coming*. 3rd ed. Chicago: Revell, 1908.
Blaising, Craig A. "Premillennialism." In *Three Views of the Millennium and Beyond*, edited by Stanly N. Gundry and Darrell L. Bock, 212–27. Grand Rapids: Zondervan, 1999.
Blaising, Craig A., and Darrell L. Bock. *Progressive Dispensationalism*. Wheaton, IL: BridgePoint, 1993.
Blaising, Craig A., and Darrell L. Bock, eds., *Dispensationalism, Israel and the Church: The Search for a Definition*. Grand Rapids: Zondervan, 2010.
Blomberg, Craig L. *From Pentecost to Patmos: An Introduction to Acts through Revelation*. Nashville: B&H Academic, 2006.
———. "The Posttribulationism of the New Testament: Leaving 'Left Behind' Behind." In *A Case for Historic Premillennialism: An Alternative to "Left Behind" Eschatology*, edited by Craig L. Blomberg and Sung Wook Chung, 61–88. Grand Rapids: Baker Academic, 2009.
Blomberg, Craig L., and Sung Wook Chung, eds. *A Case for Historic Premillennialism: An Alternative to "Left Behind" Eschatology*. Grand Rapids: Baker Academic, 2009.

BIBLIOGRAPHY

Bock, Darrell L. "Covenant in Progressive Dispensationalism." In *Three Central Issues in Contemporary Dispensatlionalism: A Comparison of Traditional and Progressive Views*, edited by Herbert W. Bateman, 169-203. Grand Rapids: Kregel, 1999.

———. "Summary Essay." In *Three Views of the Millennium and Beyond*, edited by Stanly N. Gundry and Darrell L. Bock, 279-303. Grand Rapids: Zondervan, 1999.

———. "Why I Am a Dispensationalist with a Small 'd.'" *JETS* 41 (1998) 383-98.

Chafer, Lewis Sperry. *Dispensationalism*. Fort Worth, TX: Exegetica, 1951.

———. *Systematic Theology*. 4 vols. 1948. Reprint. Grand Rapids: Kregel, 1993.

Cho, David Yonggi. *The Apocalyptic Prophecy: Reconciling Today's Global Events with End-Time Prophecy*. Lake Mary, FL: Charisma House, 1998.

———. *Daniel: Insight on the Life and Dreams of the Prophet from Babylon*. Lake Mary, FL: Creation House, 1990.

———. *Revelation: Visions of Our Ultimate Victory in Christ*. Nashville: Thomas Nelson, 1992.

Chung, Sung Wook. "Toward the Reformed and Covenantal Theology of Premillennialism: A Proposal." In *A Case for Historic Premillennialism: An Alternative to "Left Behind" Eschatology*, edited by Craig L. Blomberg and Sung Wook Chung, 133-46. Grand Rapids: Baker, 2009.

———. "Who Are the Two Witnesses in Revelation 11? An Integration of Western and Asian Proposals." Paper presented at the Biblical Studies Conference, Denver Seminary, Littleton, CO, February 2009.

Couch, Mal, ed. *Dictionary of Premillennial Theology*. Grand Rapids: Kregel, 1996.

Diprose, Ronald E. *Israel and the Church: The Origins and Effects of Replacement Theology*. Downers Grove, IL: InterVarsity, 2004.

Erickson, Millard J. *A Basic Guide to Eschatology: Making Sense of the Millennium*. Grand Rapids: Baker, 1999.

———. *Christian Theology*. 2nd ed. Grand Rapids: Baker, 1998.

Fairbairn, Donald. "Contemporary Millennial/Tribulational Debates: Whose Side Was the Early Church On?" In *A Case for Historic Premillennialism: An Alternative to "Left Behind" Eschatology*, edited by Craig L. Blomberg and Sung Wook Chung, 105-32. Grand Rapids: Baker Academic, 2009.

Fee, Gordon D. *Revelation: A New Covenant Commentary*. New Covenant Commentary Series 18. Eugene, OR: Wipf & Stock, 2011.

Feinberg, Paul D. "The Case for the Pretribulation Rapture Position." In *The Rapture: Pre-, Mid-, or Posttribulational?* by Gleason L. Archer Jr. et al., 45-86. Contemporary Evangelical Perspectives. Grand Rapids: Zondervan, 1984.

Field, Marion. *John Nelson Darby: Prophetic Pioneer*. Godalming, UK: Highland Books, 2008.

BIBLIOGRAPHY

Gaebelein, Arno C. *Current Events in the Light of the Bible.* 1914. Reprint. South Yarra, Australia: Leopold Classic Library, 2007.

———. *The Prophet Daniel.* New York: Publication Office "Our Hope," 1911.

———. *The Revelation: An Analysis and Exposition of the Last Book of the Bible.* 1915. Reprint. Neptune, NJ: Loizeaux Brothers, 1960.

Gregg, Steve, ed. *Revelation: Four Views; A Parallel Commentary.* Nashville: Thomas Nelson, 1997.

Grudem, Wayne A. *Systematic Theology: An Introduction to Biblical Doctrine.* Grand Rapids: Zondervan, 1994.

Gundry, Robert H. *The Church and the Tribulation: A Biblical Examination of Posttribulationism.* Grand Rapids: Zondervan, 1973.

———. *First the Antichrist: Why Christ Won't Come before the Antichrist Does.* Grand Rapids: Baker, 1977.

Hendriksen, William. *More than Conquerors: An Interpretation of the Book of Revelation.* Grand Rapids: Baker, 1939.

Hess, Richard S. "The Future Written in the Past: The Old Testament and the Millennium." In *A Case for Historic Premillennialism: An Alternative to "Left Behind" Eschatology,* edited by Craig L. Blomberg and Sung Wook Chung, 23–36. Grand Rapids: Baker Academic, 2009.

Hultberg, Alan, ed. *Three Views on the Rapture: Pretribulation, Prewrath, or Posttribulation.* Rev. ed. Counterpoints: Bible and Theology. Grand Rapids: Zondervan, 2010.

Ironside, Harry A. *Not Wrath But Rapture: Will the Church Participate in the Great Tribulation?* Neptune, NJ: Loizeaux Brothers, 1941.

———. *Revelation.* 1920. Reprint. Grand Rapids: Kregel, 2004.

Kim, Hyung Tae. *Go into the Land I Am About to Give.* Seoul: Bomun, 1990.

———. *Revelation Bible Study.* Seoul: Zion Bible College, 1994.

———. *What Will Take Place.* Seoul: Voice, 2000.

Keener, Craig S. *Revelation.* NIV Application Commentary. Grand Rapids: Zondervan, 2000.

Koester, Craig R. *Revelation and the End of All Things.* Grand Rapids: Eerdmans, 2001.

Koester, Craig R. *Revelation.* The Anchor Yale Bible. New Haven: Yale University Press, 2014.

Ladd, George E. *The Blessed Hope: A Biblical Study of the Second Advent and the Rapture.* Grand Rapids: Eerdmans, 1990.

LaHaye, Tim, and Jerry B. Jenkins. *Left Behind Series.* Wheaton, IL: Tyndale House, 1995–2007.

Laurent, Bob. *Watchman Nee: Man of Suffering.* Heroes of the Faith. Uhrichsville, OH: Barbour, 1998.

Lee, Gwang Bok. *The Complete Collection of Revelation and Biblical Eschatology.* Seoul: Hindol, 2013.

Lewis, C. S. *Mere Christianity.* New York: Macmillian, 1952.

BIBLIOGRAPHY

Lewis, Gordon R., and Bruce A. Demarest. *Integrative Theology.* 3 vols. Grand Rapids: Zondervan, 1987-94.

Lindsey, Hal. *The 1980s: Countdown to Armageddon.* King of Prussia, PA: Westgate, 1980.

———. *The Rapture: Truth or Consequences.* New York: Bantam, 1983.

Lindsey, Hal, with C. C. Carlson. *The Late Great Planet Earth.* Grand Rapids: Zondervan, 1970.

MacArthur, John F. *Because the Time Is Near: John MacArthur Explains the Book of Revelation.* Chicago: Moody, 2007.

———. *The Second Coming: Signs of Christ's Return and the End of Age.* Wheaton, IL: Crossway, 1999.

MacArthur, John F., and Richard Mayhue, eds. *Christ's Prophetic Plans: Futuristic Premillennial Primer.* Chicago: Moody, 2012.

Mangum, R. Todd, and Mark Sweetnam. *The Scofield Bible: Its History and Impact on the Evangelical Church.* Colorado Springs: Paternoster, 2009.

Marsden, George M. *Fundamentalism and American Culture: The Shaping of Twentieth Century Evangelicalism, 1870-1925.* New York: Oxford University Press, 1980.

Mathewson, David L. *A New Heaven and a New Earth: The Meaning and Function of the Old Testament in Revelation 21.1—22.5.* London: Bloomsbury T. & T. Clark, 2003.

———. "A Re-examination of the Millennium in Rev 20:1-6: Consummation and Recapitulation." *JETS* 44 (2001) 237-51.

———. *Revelation: A Handbook on the Greek Text.* Waco, TX: Baylor, 2016.

McLaughlin, William G. *Revivals, Awakenings and Reform: An Essay on Religious and Social Change in America, 1607-1977.* Chicago: University of Chicago Press, 1980.

McKelvey, R. J. "The Millennium and the Second Coming." In *Studies in the Book of Revelation*, edited by Steve Moyise, 85-100. Edinburgh: T. & T. Clark, 2001.

Michaels, J. Ramsey. *Interpreting the Book of Revelation.* Grand Rapids: Baker, 1992.

Min, Byeong Seok. *The Reformed Premillennialism.* Seoul: Bamjoongsori Theological Institute, 2016.

Montgomery, J. W. "Millennium." In *The International Standard Bible Encyclopedia*, edited by Geoffrey W. Bromiley, 356-61. Vol. 3. Rev. ed. Grand Rapids: Eerdmans, 1986.

Moo, Douglas J. "A Case for the Posttribulation Rapture." In *Three Views on the Rapture: Pretribulation, Prewrath, or Posttribulation*, edited by Alan Hultberg, 185-241. Rev. ed. Counterpoints: Bible and Theology. Grand Rapids: Zondervan, 2010.

Morris, Leon. *Revelation.* TNTC. Rev. ed. Leicester, UK: IVP, 1987.

Mounce, Robert H. *The Book of Revelation.* NICNT. Grand Rapids: Eerdmans, 1977.

BIBLIOGRAPHY

Mounce, Robert H. *The Book of Revelation*. Rev. ed. NICNT. Grand Rapids: Eerdmans, 1998.
Osborne, Grant R. *Revelation*. Baker Exegetical Commentary on the New Testament. Grand Rapids: Baker Academic, 2002.
Park, Hyung Ryong. *The Doctrine of the Next World*. Vol. 7, *Dogmatics*. Seoul: Christian Education Institute, 1973.
———. *Dogmatics*. 7 vols. Seoul: Christian Education Institute, 1964–73.
Park, Soo Am. *Revelation: New Testament Commentary*. Seoul: Christian Literature Society of Korea, 1998.
Pentecost, J. Dwight. *Things to Come: A Study in Biblical Eschatology*. Findlay, OH: Dunham, 1958.
———. *Thy Kingdom Come: Tracing God's Kingdom Program and Covenant Promises Throughout History*. Grand Rapids: Kregel, 1995.
Reetzke, James. *M. E. Barber: A Seed Sown in China*. Chicago: Chicago Bibles & Books, 2005.
Ryrie, Charles C. *The Basis of the Premillennial Faith*. Neptune, NJ: Loizeaux Brothers, 1981.
———. *Come Quickly, Lord Jesus: What You Need to Know about the Rapture*. Rev. ed. Eugene, OR: Harvest House, 1996.
———. *Dispensationalism*. Chicago: Moody, 1995.
———. *Dispensationalism Today*. Chicago: Moody, 1965.
———. *Revelation*. Chicago: Moody, 1968.
Saucy, Robert L. *The Case for Progressive Dispensationalism: The Interface between Dispensational and Non-Dispensational Theology*. Grand Rapids: Zondervan, 1993.
Schnackenburg, Rudolph. *God's Rule and Kingdom*. New York: Herder and Herder, 1963.
Scofield, C. I., ed. *Scofield Reference Bible*. New York: Oxford University Press, 1909.
Siew, Antoninus King Wai. *The War between the Two Beasts and the Two Witnesses: A Chiastic Reading Revelation 11:1—14:5*. Library of New Testament Studies 283. London: T. & T. Clark, 2005.
Vlach, Michael J. *The Church as a Replacement of Israel: An Analysis of Supersessionism*. Edition Israelogie 2. New York: Lang, 2009.
———. *Has the Church Replaced Israel? A Theological Evaluation*. Nashville: B&H Academic, 2010.
Wainwright, Arthur. *Mysterious Apocalypse: Interpreting the Book of Revelation*. Nashville: Abingdon, 1993.
Walvoord, John F. *The Blessed Hope and the Tribulation: A Historical and Biblical Study of Posttribulationism*. Grand Rapids: Zondervan, 1976.
———. *Daniel: The Key to Prophetic Revelation*. Chicago: Moody, 1971.
———. *The Millennial Kingdom*. Rev. ed. Grand Rapids: Zondervan, 1983.
———. *The Rapture Question*. Rev. ed. Grand Rapids: Zondervan, 1979.
———. *The Revelation of Jesus Christ*. Chicago: Moody, 1966.

BIBLIOGRAPHY

Weremchuk, Max S. *John Nelson Darby: A Biography*. Neptune, NJ: Loizeaux Brothers, 1993.

Witherington, Ben, III. *Jesus, Paul and the End of the World: A Comparative Study in New Testament Eschatology*. Downers Grove, IL: InterVarsity, 1992.

———. *Revelation*. New Cambridge Bible Commentary. Cambridge: Cambridge University Press, 2003.

Wu, Dongsheng John. *Understanding Watchman Nee: Spirituality, Knowledge, and Formation*. Eugene, OR: Wipf & Stock, 2012.

Author Index

Allison, Gregg R., 11, 11n15, 13, 14n23–16n28, 16n30, 17, 17n32–33, 18
Alsted, Johann H., 16–18, 16n29
Augustine, 14–15

Barber, Margaret E., 50, 50n24
Beasley-Murray, George R., 24, 24n48
Blomberg, Craig L., 1, 2n1, 4n3, 21–23, 34n5, 98, 108, 108n33, 109n34
Brooks, James H., 43–44

Calvin, John, 15–16, 18, 43, 50
Carlson, C.C., 48n20
Carson, D.A., 21
Chafer, Lewis S., 19, 45, 45n15
Cho, David (Paul) Yonggi, 51, 51n26–27, 90
Chung, Sung Wook, 2n1, 97n8
Couch, Mal 18n38

Darby, John N., 19, 42–43, 42n10, 45, 50–51
Demarest, Bruce A., 8n6, 10, 10n12, 18n37, 26, 35n6
Diprose, Ronald E., 40n9
Drummond, Henry, 18
Erdman, Charles, 20, 91, 94

Erickson, Millard J., 25–26, 25n51, 26n52

Fairbairn, Donald, 8n6
Fee, Gordon D., 3n2, 78, 78n9, 80–83, 81n21–22, 81n27, 83n33, 102, 102n20
Field, Marion, 42n10

Gaebelein, Arno C., 44, 45n15, 108, 108n30
Gregg, Steve, 108, 108n31
Grudem, Wayne A., 26
Gundry, Robert H., 21, 22n41–42, 23n43–44

Hendriksen, William, 108, 108n32
Hess, Richard S. 24–25, 24n49
Hippolytus, 11–12, 11n16, 12n17, 87n42
Holmes, Michael W., 9n7–8

Irenaeus, 8, 10–11, 10n13, 11n14
Ironside, Henry A., 46, 46n17–18

Keener, Craig S., 24, 24n47
Kim, Hyung Tae, 90, 95, 96, 116, 118, 125

Lactantius, 13, 13n21–22

133

AUTHOR INDEX

Ladd, George E., 5n4, 20, 54, 94–95, 98, 108, 115
LaHaye and Jenkins, 19, 30, 30n1, 49, 49n21
Laurent, Bob, 50n23
Lee, Gwang Bok, 90, 99, 109, 110, 116–18, 124–25
Lewis, Gordon R., 10, 26, 71, 102
Lewis, C.S., 40, 40n8
Lindsey, Hal, 19, 48n20, 40
Luther, Martin, 15–16

MacArthur, John F., 50
Mangum, and Sweetnam, 44n13
Marsden, 44n13
Martyr, Justin, 9–10, 9n9–10, 10n11
Mede, Joseph, 16–17, 16n31, 18
Min, Byeong Seok, 90, 94, 99, 100, 116, 118
Montgomery, J.W., 17n34, 17n36
Moo, Douglas J., 22, 22n40
Moody, Dwight L., 19, 43–44, 46
Mounce, Robert H., 3n2, 23, 39n7, 75n5, 80, 80n17, 84, 84n39–40, 102, 102n19, 107, 107n29

Nee, Watchman, 50–51, 50n23, 51n25

Osborne, Grant R., 24, 24n46

Papias, 8–9, 9n7–8,
Park, Hyung Ryong, 89–91, 111, 115, 116, 118
Pentecost, J. Dwight, 47
Polycarp, 8–10

Reetzke, James, 50n24
Ryrie, Charles C., 47–48, 65n39, 109n35

Scofield, C.I., 19, 44n13, 43–46, 43n11

Tertullian, 12–13, 12n18–20
Tyconius, 14–15

Vlach, Michael J., 32n2–3

Walvoord, John F., 35n6, 46–47, 46n19, 109n36
Weremchuk, Max S., 42n10

Scripture Index

Extra-biblical Works

2 Baruch

29:3—30:1	85
40:1-4	85
72:2—73:3	85

1 Enoch

10:4-6	81
10:11-13	81
53:3-5	81
54:1-6	81
93:3-17	85

4 Ezra

7:26-44	85
12:31-34	85

Old Testament

Genesis

1-3	121
1:26-28	6
1:28	97, 112, 116
2:15-17	97
2:16-17	116
3	76
3:15	6

Psalm

2	55, 57, 63
90:4	87
110	55
110:1	57

Isaiah

2:1-4	16
2:2-4	57
2:4	97
9:7	57
11:6-9	13
14:3-4	98
24:21-22	81
34:1-17	16
60	57, 62
65	62, 84, 120
65:17-25	106, 114
65:17-20	63
65:23	98, 112
65:25	98

SCRIPTURE INDEX

Ezekiel

36–37	120
37	62
37:24–28	57
40–48	62
44:25	63
44:27	63

Daniel

7:14	63
7:27	63
9	25, 46, 51
9:24–27	35
9:27	36
12:2	63

Micah

4:3	98
4:7	57

Zechariah

14	62
14:16–17	98

New Testament

Matthew

13	24, 58
19:28	61
22:30	112, 117
24	50
24:9–12	93
24:14	93
24:15	36
24:21–24	93
24:21	10

Mark

13:9–22	93
13:10	93

Luke

21:20–28	93
21:22–24	93

Acts

2:34–35	55

Romans

11	59
11:25	93
11:26	93

1 Corinthians

6:2	61
15:20–26	117
15:22–26	103, 105
15:22–24	94, 116
15:22–23	104
15:23–25	62
15:23	103, 104
15:24	62, 94, 103
15:25	62
15:26	103
15:51–52	105

Galatians

3–4	59
3:28	40

Ephesians

1:20–23	55
2:14–18	40

SCRIPTURE INDEX

1 Thessalonians

1:10	36
4:13–18	36, 104, 105, 117
4:16	105, 117
5:9	37

2 Thessalonians

2:3	93

1 Timothy

4:1	93

2 Timothy

3:1–5	93

Hebrews

1:5	55
1:13	55

1 Peter

5:8	3, 34

2 Peter

2:4	81
3:13	114

Jude

6	81

Revelation

1:12–16	71, 72
1:20	72
2–3	74, 110
2:11	74
2:26–27	74
3:21	74
4:1	37
5:6–7	71
6–19	33
6	75
6:9	74
6:10	74, 78
6:11	101
7	107, 115, 118
11:1—14:5	88
11–13	75
11	99, 108, 109, 114, 115, 116, 118
11:2	75
11:3	75
11:7–12	102
11:7	109
11:11–13	76
11:11	76, 109
11:12–13	76
11:15	77
11:18	76, 79
12–13	76
12:6	75
12:9	76
12:10	75, 76
12:12	75
12:14	75, 114
13	5, 38
13:5	75
13:10	5, 37
14	107, 118
17:10–13	48
17:12	72
17:14	104
18:8	78
18:20	78
18:24	82
19–22	120
19:2	78
19:11—22:5	71, 73, 77
19:11—21:8	61

Revelation (continued)

19–20	xii, 4, 34		76, 79, 80, 81, 82, 84, 85, 86, 94, 111, 123, 125, 126
19:11—20:15	76, 77, 78, 79, 82	20:4–5	101, 102, 104
19	4, 34, 35, 124	20:4	61, 74, 79, 98, 101, 109, 115
19:11–21	61, 62, 76, 77, 78, 79, 86, 121, 124	20:5	61, 102
		20:6	98
19:11–16	71	20:7–11	78, 86
19:11	77, 78	20:7–10	4, 34, 35, 76, 78, 80, 86, 123, 124
19:14	104, 109		
19:15	112		
19:19–21	4, 34	20:7–8	81
20–22	62	20:8–11	63
20:11—22:5	77	20:8	112
20	4, 32, 34, 53, 60, 61, 63, 64, 67, 70, 71, 74, 79, 110, 113, 115, 119, 120	20:10	4, 34
		20:11–15	76, 78, 79, 86
		20:11–14	61
		20:14	74, 103
		21–22	54, 59, 60, 64, 67, 68, 70, 84, 98, 113, 114, 117, 125
20:1–6	xii, 2, 4, 32, 33, 34, 35, 62, 72, 78, 82, 119, 120, 121		
		21:1—22:5	61, 62, 67, 68, 69, 70, 77, 84, 85, 86, 121, 124, 125
20:1–3	2, 32, 61, 78, 79, 80, 86, 97		
20:3	3		
20:4–6	xi, xii, 3, 33, 53, 59, 60, 62, 65, 67, 68, 69, 71, 72, 73, 74,	21	110
		21:1	125
		21:2	113
		22:16	5, 38

www.ingramcontent.com/pod-product-compliance
Lightning Source LLC
Chambersburg PA
CBHW022127160426
43197CB00009B/1182